Personal Best

A2 Elementary

Student's Book and Workbook combined edition **B**

Series Editor
Jim Scrivener

Student's Book Author
Louis Rogers

Workbook Author
Genevieve White

STUDENT'S BOOK CONTENTS

		LANGUAGE			SKILLS	
		GRAMMAR	PRONUNCIATION	VOCABULARY		
7 Food and drink		countable and uncountable nouns + some/any	some/any, weak form of	food and drink, containers and portions	READING — an article about what people eat for lunch around the world; skimming a text; pronouns and possessive adjectives	SPEAKING — in a restaurant; asking politely for something. **PERSONAL BEST** — ordering food in a restaurant
7A Food to your door	p58	quantifiers: (how) much/many, a lot of, a few, a little				
7B Stopping for lunch	p60					
7C Are you hungry?	p62					
7D Out for dinner	p64					
8 In the past		past of be, there was/there were; simple past: irregular verbs; simple past: regular verbs and past time expressions	was and were; -ed endings	inventions; life stages; irregular verbs	LISTENING — a video about our favorite inventions and inspirations; listening for numbers, dates, and prices; phrases	WRITING — planning and making notes; sequencers. **PERSONAL BEST** — a story about an experience you had
8A Technology through the ages	p66					
8B Life stories	p68					
8C Life in the 1980s	p70					
8D What happened to you?	p72					
7 and 8 REVIEW and PRACTICE	p74					
9 Education, education!		simple past: questions; verb patterns: verb + to infinitive	intonation in questions; 'd like and like	school subjects and education; resolutions	READING — an article about different education experiences; understanding words that you don't know; because and so	SPEAKING — making suggestions; sounding sympathetic. **PERSONAL BEST** — describing and responding to problems
9A School days	p76					
9B Lifelong learning	p78					
9C Change your life	p80					
9D What's the problem?	p82					
10 People		comparative adjectives; superlative adjectives	-er endings; superlative adjectives	adjectives to describe places; describing appearance; personality adjectives	LISTENING — a video about changing our appearance; listening for detailed information (1); weak forms	WRITING — writing a description of a person; clauses with when. **PERSONAL BEST** — a description of someone you admire
10A First dates	p84					
10B You look so different!	p86					
10C The yearbook	p88					
10D Someone that I admire	p90					
9 and 10 REVIEW and PRACTICE	p92					
11 On the move		have to/don't have to; be going to, future time expressions	have to/has to; sentence stress	travel and transportation; vacation activities	READING — an article about the unusual way Jordan Axani found a travel partner; reading for detail; adverbs of probability	SPEAKING — arriving at a hotel; checking information. **PERSONAL BEST** — a conversation at a hotel reception
11A Getting to work	p94					
11B Looking for Elizabeth Gallagher	p96					
11C Road trip	p98					
11D In a hotel	p100					
12 Enjoy yourself!		present perfect with ever and never; present perfect and simple past	sentence stress; vowels	entertainment; opinion adjectives	LISTENING — a video about books that have become movies; listening for detailed information (2); linking consonants and vowels	WRITING — writing and replying to an invitation; articles: a/an, the, or no article. **PERSONAL BEST** — an invitation to a party and a reply
12A Going out	p102					
12B The book was better!	p104					
12C A famous voice	p106					
12D Would you like to come?	p108					
11 and 12 REVIEW and PRACTICE	p110					

Grammar practice p124   Vocabulary practice p147   Communication practice p162   Irregular verbs p176

WORKBOOK CONTENTS

		LANGUAGE		SKILLS	
		GRAMMAR	PRONUNCIATION	VOCABULARY		

7 Food and drink
- 7A p38
- 7B p39
- 7C p40
- 7D p41

GRAMMAR	PRONUNCIATION	VOCABULARY	READING	SPEAKING
• countable and uncountable nouns + some/any • quantifiers: (how) much/many, a lot of, a few, a little	• some/any • weak form of	• food and drink • containers and portions	• skimming a text	• asking politely for something

7 — REVIEW and PRACTICE p42

8 In the past
- 8A p44
- 8B p45
- 8C p46
- 8D p47

GRAMMAR	PRONUNCIATION	VOCABULARY	LISTENING	WRITING
• past of be, there was, there were, and simple past: irregular verbs • past simple: regular verbs and past time expressions	• was and were • -ed endings	• inventions • life stages	• listening for numbers, dates, and prices	• planning and making notes

8 — REVIEW and PRACTICE p48

9 Education, education!
- 9A p50
- 9B p51
- 9C p52
- 9D p53

GRAMMAR	PRONUNCIATION	VOCABULARY	READING	SPEAKING
• past simple: questions • verb patterns: verb + to + infinitive	• intonation in questions • 'd like and like	• school subjects and education • resolutions	• understanding words that you don't know	• sounding sympathetic

9 — REVIEW and PRACTICE p54

10 People
- 10A p56
- 10B p57
- 10C p58
- 10D p59

GRAMMAR	PRONUNCIATION	VOCABULARY	LISTENING	WRITING
• comparative adjectives • superlative adjectives	• -er endings • superlative adjectives	• adjectives to describe places • describing appearance • personality adjectives	• listening for detailed information (1)	• writing a description of a person

10 — REVIEW and PRACTICE p60

11 On the move
- 11A p62
- 11B p63
- 11C p64
- 11D p65

GRAMMAR	PRONUNCIATION	VOCABULARY	READING	SPEAKING
• have to/don't have to • be going to, future time expressions	• have to/has to • sentence stress	• travel and transportation • vacation activities	• reading for detail	• checking information

11 — REVIEW and PRACTICE p66

12 Enjoy yourself!
- 12A p68
- 12B p69
- 12C p70
- 12D p71

GRAMMAR	PRONUNCIATION	VOCABULARY	LISTENING	WRITING
• present perfect with ever and never • present perfect and simple past	• sentence stress • vowels	• entertainment • opinion adjectives	• listening for detailed information (2)	• writing and replying to an invitation

12 — REVIEW and PRACTICE p72

Writing practice p77

UNIT 7

Food and drink

LANGUAGE countable and uncountable nouns + *some/any* ■ food and drink

7A Food to your door

1 A Discuss the questions in pairs.

1 Where do you usually go food shopping?
2 How often do you buy food?
3 Do you enjoy food shopping? Why/Why not?

B Look at the pictures on the page. Which items of food can you name?

Go to Vocabulary practice: food and drink, page 147

2 Read the text. What types of food are very popular in food boxes?

What should we have for dinner?

Do you hate supermarkets? Do you like eating healthy meals? A lot of companies in different countries now deliver food boxes to your house. You can find boxes with all different types of food: fresh fruit and vegetables, meat and fish, vegetarian and vegan food, and even desserts, cookies, and cakes. Fruit and vegetables are very popular, especially if it's the season when they're fresh. You usually can't choose the food in the box – it's a surprise!

3 A ▶ 7.2 Listen to James and Fran. What do they cook for their dinner?

B ▶ 7.2 Listen again. Which two types of food aren't in the food box?

fruit   potatoes   eggs   peas   rice
beef   onions   peppers

4 A ▶ 7.3 Listen and complete the sentences.

1 We need _____ pepper.
2 There's _____ beef.
3 There isn't _____ rice.
4 You have _____ tomatoes, strawberries, and potatoes.
5 Are there _____ onions?
6 There aren't _____ peppers.

B Read the sentences again and complete the rules with *singular* or *plural*. Then read the Grammar box.

1 Uncountable nouns like *rice* and *beef* only have a _____ form.
2 Countable nouns like *tomato* and *onion* can be singular or _____.
3 We use *some* and *any* with uncountable and _____ countable nouns.

countable and uncountable nouns + *some/any* ■ food and drink   **LANGUAGE**   **7A**

📖 **Grammar** countable and uncountable nouns + *some/any*

Countable nouns:

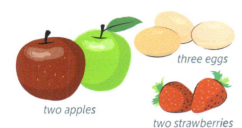

two apples
three eggs
two strawberries

Uncountable nouns:

rice
meat
pasta

There are **some** onions.
Are there **any** tomatoes?
We don't need **any** potatoes.

There's **some** fruit.
Do we have **any** pasta?
There isn't **any** juice.

Go to Grammar practice: countable and uncountable nouns + *some/any*, page 124

5 A ▶ 7.5 **Pronunciation:** *some/any* Listen to the sentences. How do we say *some* and *any*? Are they stressed?
1 I have some fruit in my bag.
2 We need some carrots.
3 There are some crackers on the plate.
4 We don't have any bread.
5 I don't want any peas.
6 Is there any milk?

B ▶ 7.5 Say the sentences. Listen again, check, and repeat.

6 A Look at the pictures and name the items. Are they countable (C) or uncountable (U)?

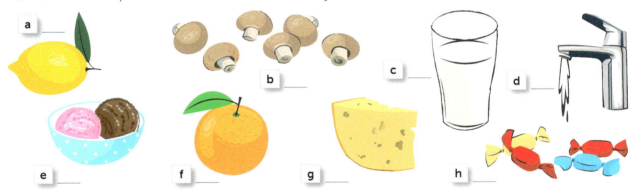

a
b
c
d
e
f
g
h

B In pairs, make sentences about the food and drink in 6A. Use *a*, *an*, or *some*.
There are some mushrooms.

7 A Imagine you are preparing a fresh-food box for a family. Choose the following food and drink to go in it:

(three types of fruit) (three types of vegetables) (some protein (meat, fish, etc.)) (something sweet)

B Guess what's in your partner's box. Ask questions with *Is there/Are there ...?* Who can guess the most items?
A *Is there any cheese?*   B *No, there's not. My turn. Are there any strawberries?*
A *Yes, there are!*

Go to Communication practice: Student A page 162, Student B page 171

8 Ask and answer the questions in pairs.
1 What do you usually have for breakfast, lunch, and dinner?
2 What food do you need for your favorite meal?
3 What food is in your fridge at home right now?

Personal Best Think of someone you know and make the perfect food box for him/her. Describe it.

7 SKILLS READING skimming a text ■ pronouns and possessive adjectives

7B Stopping for lunch

1 **A** How important is it for you to stop for a lunch break every day? Mark the line.

1   2   3   4   5   6   7   8   9   10

Very important   Not important at all

B In pairs, discuss the questions. How long is your lunch break? Where do you usually have lunch?

Skill | skimming a text

When we skim a text, we read it quickly to understand the main ideas.
- Read the first sentence of each paragraph to get an idea of the topic.
- Read the rest of each paragraph quickly. Don't worry if you don't understand every word.
- Try to understand the general idea or ideas in the text.

2 Read the Skill box. Skim the text and match the countries with the sentences.

the U.S.   Italy   Kenya

1 People often have lunch with their colleagues. _____
2 People often have a quick lunch. _____
3 Lunch breaks in cities are different from in the country. _____

3 Read the text again and answer the questions.
1 What do people like in their sandwiches in the U.S.?
2 What does Carla do when she has lunch?
3 Why is lunch very important in Kenya?
4 Where does Joseph like sitting for lunch?
5 What happens to a lot of stores in small towns in Italy at lunchtime?
6 What does Andrea sometimes do after lunch?

4 Match the places from the text with the sentences.
1 A lot of working people in the U.S. eat their lunch here. _____, _____
2 People in the U.S. often buy sandwiches here. _____, _____, _____
3 A lot of popular food in Kenya comes from here. _____
4 Italians in the country often eat their lunch here. _____

5 In pairs, discuss the people in the text. Whose lunch break is similar to yours? Which do you think is the best and why?

Text builder | pronouns and possessive adjectives

We use pronouns and possessive adjectives to avoid repeating nouns and names:
I usually buy a **sandwich**. I eat **it** at my desk.
Working people usually have a long, sociable lunch. **They** often go to **their** favorite restaurant.

6 Read the Text builder. Look at the sentences from the text. What do the underlined pronouns and possessive adjectives refer to?
1 My lunch break is an hour, but <u>it</u>'s longer on Fridays.
2 The quality of the food is very important to Italians, even if <u>their</u> lunch break is short.
3 My wife is an excellent cook. <u>She</u> usually makes some pasta with beef and tomato sauce.

7 In pairs, think about different people and their jobs in your country. How long is their lunch break? Where do they go for lunch? What do you think they have?

skimming a text ■ pronouns and possessive adjectives   READING   SKILLS   7B

Lunches around the world

THE U.S.
In the U.S., a lot of working people take a short lunch break. They eat lunch in their office or even at their desk. Sandwiches are the most popular lunch, and they're often filled with cheese or meat, such as chicken. People bring their own sandwiches or buy them from a supermarket, delicatessen, or café. A lot of places also sell salads and soup to take out.

KENYA
In Kenya, lunch is a very important meal because people leave home very early, and they don't have time for breakfast. Working people usually have a long, sociable lunch. They often go to their favorite restaurant with their colleagues. People eat a lot of fish, and the most popular dishes come from the west of Kenya.

ITALY
In small towns and villages in Italy, people usually take a long lunch break. Stores and businesses close for two or three hours, and families have a big lunch together at home. It's different in big cities – people take a shorter lunch break and usually don't go home. The quality of the food is very important to Italians, even if their lunch break is short.

CARLA, 34, ACCOUNTANT
"I rarely take more than ten to fifteen minutes to eat my lunch. I usually buy a sandwich from a coffee shop near the office. I then eat it at my desk and read the news on the Internet. After that, I continue working."

JOSEPH, 39, IT WORKER
"My lunch break is an hour, but it's longer on Fridays. I usually go for lunch with some friends from work, and we like sitting outside in the sun to eat. It's nice to have lunch together. I usually order the same dish: fish with vegetables in a creamy sauce."

ANDREA, 43, STORE OWNER
"I always close my store for lunch and eat with my family. My wife is an excellent cook. She usually makes some pasta with beef and tomato sauce, and then we have chicken or fish with fresh vegetables. I sometimes have a nap (a short sleep) after lunch. I open the store again at 4 p.m."

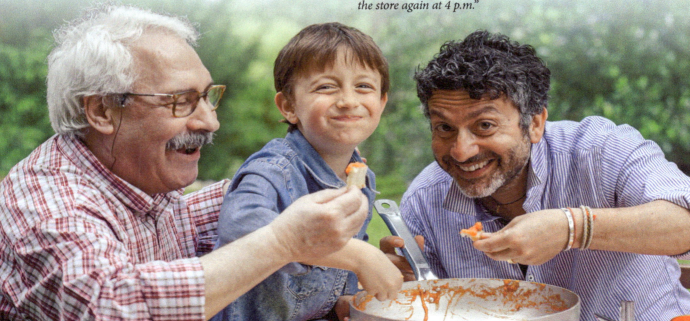

Personal Best   Write a paragraph about a typical lunch on a work day for you.

7 LANGUAGE
quantifiers: *(how) much, (how) many, a lot of, a few, a little* ■ containers and portions

7C Are you hungry?

1 Look at the picture and discuss the questions in pairs.
  1 What can and can't you eat or drink when you're on a diet?
  2 Do you know any unusual diets?

2 A Read the text. Why is the diet called the "5:2 diet"? Do you think it is a good idea?
  B Complete the chart with the food and drink that Gary eats every week.

	Vegetables	Fruit	Meat	Dairy products	Drinks	Other food
Five days a week						
Two days a week						

The 5:2 diet

Do you know about the 5:2 diet?

For some people, this amazing diet really works. On the 5:2 diet, you can eat normally for five days a week. You are only on the diet for two days a week, but, on those two days, you can only eat 500 calories a day if you're a woman and 600 if you're a man.

How much is 600 calories? Here are some examples:

1 large burger   2 small bars of chocolate

3 bags of potato chips   2 bowls of rice

6 tins of tomatoes   6 bananas

Gary is on the 5:2 diet.

FIVE DAYS a week, he has:
● Breakfast – two eggs, three slices of toast with butter, a cup of coffee with milk and sugar
● Snack – a few cookies
● Lunch – a bag of nuts, two sandwiches
● Snack – a small bag of potato chips, a carton of juice
● Dinner – pasta with beef and tomato sauce, peas
● Drinks – five cups of coffee with sugar and milk, three bottles of cola

TWO DAYS a week, he has:
● Breakfast – a slice of toast with no butter, a cup of coffee with no milk
● Snack – water, an apple
● Lunch – salad
● Snack – an orange
● Dinner – chicken and cabbage
● Snack – a few grapes

3 A Label the items from Gary's list.

a *a slice of toast*   b _____   c _____   d _____   e _____   f _____

quantifiers: *(how) much, (how) many, a lot of, a few, a little* ■ containers and portions   **LANGUAGE 7C**

B Cover page 62 and answer the questions in pairs.
1 What do you remember about Gary's diet?
2 What can he eat two days a week?
3 What can he eat five days a week?

Go to **Vocabulary practice:** containers and portions, page 148

4 A ▶ 7.7 Listen to Gary talking to his friend Amy about his diet. Is it a "5" or a "2" day today?
B ▶ 7.7 Listen again and complete the sentences and questions.
1 I normally have a lot of _____ for breakfast.
2 How much _____ can you have?
3 I only have a little _____ – not a lot.
4 How many _____ of coffee do you have on a "5" day?
5 I don't eat much _____, and I don't eat many _____.
6 I have a few _____ in the morning for my snack.

5 A Look again at 4B and complete the sentences with *much*, *many*, and *a lot of*.
Then read the Grammar box.
1 We use *How* _____ to ask about countable nouns.
2 We use *How* _____ to ask about uncountable nouns.
3 We use _____ in affirmative sentences and questions.
4 We use _____ and _____ in negative sentences.

B Which phrase in 4B means "a large amount"? Which phrase means "a small amount"? Which phrase means "a small number"?

📖 **Grammar**   quantifiers: *(how) much, (how) many, a lot of, a few, a little*

Countable nouns:
I eat **a lot of** vegetables.
I have **a few** cookies with my coffee.
I don't eat **many** potato chips.
Do you eat **many** vegetables?
How many eggs do you eat? Not **many**./**A few**./**A lot**.

Uncountable nouns:
I eat **a lot of** fruit.
I put **a little** milk in my coffee.
I don't eat **much** meat.
Do you drink **a lot of** coffee?
How much fruit do you eat? Not **much**./**A little**./**A lot**.

Go to **Grammar practice:** quantifiers: *(how) much, (how) many, a lot of, a few, a little*, page 125

6 A ▶ 7.9 **Pronunciation:** weak form *of* Listen and repeat the phrases.
1 a lot of pasta
2 a cup of coffee
3 a bottle of water
4 a lot of salad
5 a glass of orange juice
6 a piece of cake

B ▶ 7.10 Say the sentences. Listen, check, and repeat.
1 I don't eat a lot of cookies.
2 Can I have a bag of potato chips, please?
3 There's a can of peas in the kitchen cabinet.
4 I drink a lot of coffee.

7 A Complete the questions with *How much* or *How many*.
1 _____ rice do you eat a week?
2 _____ pasta do you eat a week?
3 _____ glasses of water do you have a day?
4 _____ cups of coffee do you have a day?
5 _____ sugar do you have a week?
6 _____ cartons of juice do you buy a week?

B Ask and answer the questions in pairs.
A *How much rice do you eat a week?*   B *I have rice about once a week. How about you?*

Go to **Communication practice:** Student A page 163, Student B page 172

8 A Do you have a healthy diet? Score your typical daily diet 1–10 on the scale below.

junk food lover 1 2 3 4 5 6 7 8 9 10 healthy eater

B Compare your scale with a partner. Discuss your typical daily diet.
A *I have a pretty healthy diet. I don't eat many cookies or a lot of cake. I don't eat junk food.*
B *Me, too. I eat a lot of fresh fruit and vegetables, but I sometimes have soft drinks, such as cola.*

Personal Best Plan a new diet to help people be healthier. What can you eat and drink each day or week?

7 SKILLS SPEAKING in a restaurant ■ asking politely for something

7D Out for dinner

1 Look at pictures a–d. In which pictures are the people:

1 asking for the check? _d_
2 ordering food? ____
3 arriving at a restaurant? ____
4 reserving a table? ____

2 A ▶ 7.11 Watch or listen to the first part of *Learning Curve*. Which activity in exercise 1 do you see or hear?

B ▶ 7.11 Watch or listen again and answer the questions below.

1 What is the name of Jack and Lance's restaurant?
2 Why is the restaurant called this?
3 What day and time does Simon want to reserve a table for?
4 How many people does he want the table for?

3 ▶ 7.12 Now watch or listen to the second part of the show. Who orders the following food and drink? Write K (Kate) or S (Simon).

1 small salad   ____
2 chicken soup   ____
3 goulash with rice ____
4 chicken   ____
5 chips, peas, and carrots ____
6 chocolate ice cream   ____
7 a cup of tea   ____

Conversation builder — in a restaurant

Reserving a table:
Do you have a table for ... please?
It's for ... people.

Arriving at a restaurant:
We have a table reserved in the name of ...

Ordering food:
I'd like the (chicken), please.
I'll have ...
Could/Can I have ...?
The same for me, please./Me too.

Paying the check:
Could/Can we have the check, please?

4 A Read the Conversation builder and complete the mini-conversations.

Waiter   Hello, Harry's Restaurant. How can I help?
Dimitri   [1] _____ Saturday for lunch, please?

Dimitri   Hello. [2] _____ Aristov.
Waiter   No problem. Follow me, please.

Waiter   Would you like a starter?
Dimitri   Yes. [3] _____ the vegetable soup, please.

Waiter   And for you?
Svetlana [4] _____ the five-bean salad, please?

Svetlana [5] _____, please?
Waiter   Would you like to pay by cash or credit card?
Svetlana By card.

B In groups of three, practice saying the conversations. Take turns being the waiter, Dimitri, and Svetlana.

in a restaurant ■ asking politely for something **SPEAKING** SKILLS **7D**

5 ▶ 7.12 Watch or listen again and complete the sentences.
1 Kate doesn't want _____ or _____ in her starter.
2 Jack's goulash has _____, _____, vegetables, and spices in it.
3 Jack wants to have _____ scoops of _____.
4 Kate wants to pay by _____, but Simon wants to pay by _____.
5 Jack says that the meals are "on the _____" – it means Simon and Kate don't need to pay.

> **Skill** asking politely for something
>
> It's important to use polite forms when you ask for something.
> Instead of *I want*, use *I'd like*, *Can I have ...?* or *Could I have ...?*
> *I'd like* a cup of coffee.
> *Could I have* a large orange juice, please?
> *Can we have* three slices of cake?
>
> Use polite intonation, too.

6 **A** ▶ 7.13 Read the Skill box. Listen to three situations. Which customer is more polite, a or b?
1 ____   2 ____   3 ____

B Take turns asking and answering the waiter's questions politely. Use the food items and drinks below or your own ideas.

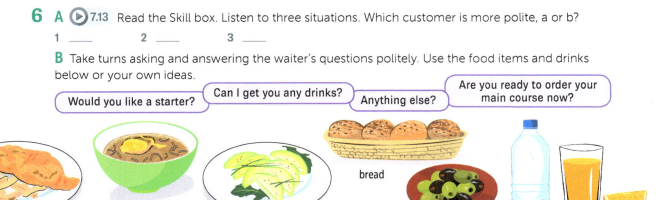

fish and chips   French onion soup   avocado salad   bread   olives   bottle of mineral water   glass of orange juice

Go to Communication practice: Student A page 163, Student B page 172

7 **A** PREPARE Look at the menu. Decide when you want to go there for a meal, with how many people, and what you would like to eat.

> ### The Bell
> **STARTERS**
> Tomato soup, Garlic mushrooms, Bean and pasta salad
>
> **MAIN COURSES**
> Roast beef, Fish of the day, Fried chicken
> All served with seasonal vegetables and a choice of French fries, boiled potatoes, or rice.
>
> **DESSERTS**
> Chocolate cake, Local cheeses, Fresh fruit, Ice cream (choice of flavors)

B PRACTICE Decide who the waiter is and who the customer is.

CUSTOMER: Call the restaurant to reserve a table. Arrive at the restaurant, order your food, and ask for the check.

WAITER: Take the telephone reservation. Welcome the customers to the restaurant, take their order, and give them the check.

C PERSONAL BEST Exchange roles and repeat the conversation. Is it easier to be the waiter or the customer? Why?

Personal Best   Plan a menu for your ideal restaurant. Describe it.

65

UNIT 8

In the past

LANGUAGE past of *be* ■ simple past: irregular verbs ■ inventions

8A Technology through the ages

1 Match the inventions with the words in the box. Do you have any of these things in your home?

video player   digital camera   microwave   TV   smartphone   CD player

a _____ b _____ c _____ d _____ e _____ f _____

Go to Vocabulary practice: inventions, page 149

2 Which inventions are important to you? Choose your top three and tell a partner.

I can't live without my smartphone, GPS, and TV.

3 A When do you think most people in the U.S. first had these things in their homes? Write *1930s*, *1960s*, or *1990s*.

washing machine _____   black-and-white TV _____   telephone _____   CD player _____
radio _____   vacuum cleaner _____   the Internet _____ freezer _____

B Read the text. When did Ethel, George, and Jessica have these things in their homes?

The 1930s

In the 1930s, life at home wasn't easy. There was a lot of housework to do, and we didn't have a lot of things to help us like we do now. There wasn't a vacuum cleaner, an electric iron, or a washing machine in our home. We didn't have a private telephone, but there was a phone that we shared with other families. We didn't make many telephone calls! We had a radio, but we didn't have a TV. In my free time (we were always busy, so there wasn't much free time!), I read a lot of books.

Ethel

The 1960s

My first house was very different from my parents' house. The furniture was very colorful, and there was a lot of technology. We had a telephone and a TV. The TV was black and white, and there were a lot of different programs, but there weren't many channels. We had some modern appliances in our kitchen – a fridge, a freezer, an electric stove, a toaster, and a washing machine, and we always had a vacuum cleaner.

George

The 1990s

In the 1990s, a lot of my friends had TVs in their bedrooms. TVs and other electrical items weren't expensive, and I had a TV and a video player in my room. I had both a cassette player and a CD player to listen to music. In 1997, I bought my first cell phone. There was a computer in our house. I didn't use it much, but in 1998, we got the Internet at home. We were so excited! I can't imagine life without the Internet now. Can you?

Jessica

past of *be* ■ simple past: irregular verbs ■ inventions   LANGUAGE **8A**

4 A Complete the sentences from the text with the correct form of *be*.
1 My first house _____ very different from my parents' house.
2 In the 1930s, life at home _____ easy.
3 We _____ so excited!
4 TVs and other electrical items _____ expensive.
5 There _____ a lot of technology.
6 There _____ many channels.

B Answer the questions. Then read the Grammar box.
1 Which are the two affirmative past forms of *be*? _____ and _____
2 What are the negative forms? _____ and _____
3 What are the past forms of *there is* and *there are*? _____ and _____

Grammar — past of *be*, there was/there were

Affirmative:
I **was** two years old in 1934.
You **were** a child in the 1960s.
Life **was** difficult in the past.
We **were** happy.

Negative:
I **wasn't** alive in 1930.
You **weren't** an adult.
It **wasn't** easy.
My parents **weren't** rich.

Past of *there is* and *there are*:
There was a TV in our living room.
There was no private telephone in our house.
There were a lot of TV programs.
There weren't many TV channels.

Go to Grammar practice: past of *be*, there was/there were, page 126

5 ▶ 8.4 **Pronunciation:** *was* and *were* Listen and repeat the sentences. Which verb forms are stressed: affirmative or negative?
1 The TV was in the living room.
2 There wasn't much free time.
3 There were two bedrooms and a bathroom.
4 Things were very different.
5 Dishwashers weren't in every home.
6 There weren't many cars.

6 A Look again at the text. Find the affirmative simple past form of these verbs.
1 have _____   2 read _____   3 buy _____   4 get _____

B Find the negative simple past form of these verbs from the text. Which verb form do we use after *didn't*? Then read the Grammar box.
1 have _____   2 make _____   3 use _____

Grammar — simple past: irregular verbs

A lot of verbs have an irregular simple past affirmative form. You need to learn them.
Affirmative:
In the 1930s, I **read** a lot of books.
We **had** a computer.

Negative:
We **didn't make** many phone calls.
I **didn't go** there much.

Go to Grammar practice: simple past: irregular verbs, page 126

7 A ▶ 8.6 Complete the text with the simple past form of the verbs in the box. Listen and check.

buy (×2)   have   not use   not have

In the 1990s, I ¹_____ a cell phone, but I ²_____ a digital camera. I ³_____ a digital camera in 2001, but then, in 2005, I ⁴_____ a smartphone, so I ⁵_____ my digital camera after that.

B Tell your partner about yourself. Use the prompts.

(In the 1990s/2000s, I had a …)   (I didn't have a …)   (I bought a …)   (I used …)

Go to Communication practice: Student A page 163, Student B page 172

8 Talk about your parents/grandparents when they were young. What did/didn't they have in their homes?

Personal Best — Think about your house when you were a child. Write about the gadgets and inventions you had.   67

8 SKILLS LISTENING — listening for numbers, dates, and prices ■ phrases ■ life stages

8B Life stories

1 Match the phrases in the box with pictures a–f.

get married   retire   go to college   be born   start school   get a job

2 Look at the chart. When do these life stages happen in your country? Discuss in pairs.

Life stage	Average age in the U.S.	Average age in the UK
start school	5 or 6	4 or 5
go to college	18 or 19	18 or 19
get married	28	31
have your first baby	26	30

In our country, people start school when they're four.

Go to Vocabulary practice: life stages, page 150

3 8.8 Watch or listen to the first part of *Learning Curve*. Choose the correct options to complete the sentences.

1 Simon talks about the invention of the *satellite* / *GPS*.
2 Kate talks about the invention of *instant coffee* / *coffee filters*.

Skill   listening for numbers, dates, and prices

We sometimes have to listen for numbers, dates, and prices:
- Practice listening to numbers regularly on the radio or on television.
- Be prepared to hear years and dates if someone is talking about the past.
- Listen for the verbs **cost** and **spend**. We often use them to talk about prices.

4 A 8.8 Read the Skill box. Watch or listen again and complete the sentences with the correct numbers, dates, and prices.

1 Simon's taxi trip took _____ minutes. It cost about £_____.
2 In 19_____, Roger Easton worked at a research center in Washington, D.C.
3 In the 19_____s, he thought of putting clocks on satellites.
4 It cost about $_____ million to build the first GPS.
5 On February _____ 1978, the first GPS satellite went into space.
6 Melitta Bentz was born on January 31, _____.
7 In the early _____th century, people used little bags to make coffee.
8 Kate usually spends £_____ when she buys a cup of coffee.

B Discuss the questions in pairs.

1 Do you use the inventions in the program? How often do you use them?
2 Which invention do you think is more important? Why?

listening for numbers, dates, and prices ■ phrases ■ life stages **LISTENING** **SKILLS** **8B**

5 **A** Look at the irregular simple past forms in the chart. Write the infinitive of each verb. Then check in the Irregular verbs list on page 176.

Infinitive	Simple past	Kate or Simon?	Infinitive	Simple past	Kate or Simon?
1	took		5	thought	
2	had		6	went	
3	told		7	made	
4	cost		8	gave	

B ▶ 8.8 Watch or listen again. Who says the irregular simple past forms in 5A? Write K (Kate) or S (Simon).

Go to Vocabulary practice: irregular verbs, page 150

6 ▶ 8.10 Watch or listen to the second part of the show. Match the people with the services that they mention. There is one service that you don't need.

cooking app   online language courses   sightseeing app   online fashion store

1 Vanessa: _____   2 Marcello: _____   3 Xander: _____

7 ▶ 8.10 Watch or listen again. Choose the correct options to complete the sentences.
1 Vanessa's birthday is on May *10th / 12th / 28th*.
2 It usually costs about *£11,000 / £23,000 / £33,000* to start a company.
3 She got her degree in *2002 / 2010 / 2012*.
4 Marcello got married *two / three / four* years ago.
5 Xander finished his invention on April *1st / 3rd / 5th*.
6 His invention costs about *$1.13 / $1.30 / $1.19*.

Listening builder   phrases

People often use set phrases when they talk, especially in informal situations. Learn them as phrases, not just individual words:
I'm just in time.   Bye for now!

8 ▶ 8.11 Read the Listening builder. Complete the sentences with the phrases in the box. Listen and check.

First of all   a cup of coffee   Of course you can!   Bye for now!   What do you do?

1 A _____   B I sell computers.
2 A Can I ask you a question?   B _____
3 A _____ See you tomorrow.   B See you!
4 A Would you like _____ and a cookie?   B Yes, please.
5 A How did you start writing books?
  B _____, I wrote a blog, and then I wrote a book.

9 In pairs, think of someone interesting that you know and talk about his/her life story.
My grandma was born in Lima in 1929. She got married to my grandfather when she was 18.

Personal Best   Think of a famous person that you know about. Write a paragraph about his/her life story.

8 LANGUAGE simple past: regular verbs and past time expressions

8C Life in the 1980s

1 A In pairs, look at the pictures. What do you know about life in the 1980s?

B Do you like the fashion and music from the 1980s? Why/Why not? Discuss in pairs.

2 Read the text. What is it about? Choose the best summary.
1. It's about a family who lived in the 1980s without any technology.
2. It's about a family who stopped living with modern technology.
3. It's about a family who didn't like 1980s technology.

BACK TO THE 1980s

In 2013, Canadian couple Blair and Morgan McMillan started to worry about their two young sons, Trey and Denton. The boys used a smartphone and a tablet, and they were always inside – they didn't want to play outside. Blair and Morgan wanted to change the situation, so they decided to live like a family in the 1980s for a year. They stopped using cell phones, tablets, the Internet, and cable TV!

Life changed a lot. Blair and Morgan stopped banking online; instead, they went to the bank in person. They used an old-fashioned camera, not a digital camera. At home, the family listened to cassettes and watched videos. There was an old games console from the 1980s, and the children played Super Mario Bros. on that. And they loved it! For their vacation, the family traveled across Canada using a map, not a GPS.

Some things were hard. Blair lost a business partner because he didn't use a computer or cell phone for his job. It was difficult for the family to communicate with their friends and relatives. They had a phone, but all their friends and family used the Internet or social media.

But a lot of things were better. The family saved a lot of money. Also, they enjoyed spending more time together in the evenings and on the weekend. The boys didn't play with their phones and computers all the time – they played with their toys in the living room, and Blair and Morgan talked on the sofa or watched 1980s TV programs.

3 Read the text again. Are the sentences true (T) or false (F)?
1. The boys liked playing outside before 2013. ____
2. Blair and Morgan stopped going to the bank in "the 1980s." ____
3. The family had a TV before 2013. ____
4. Blair didn't use modern technology in his work in "the 1980s." ____
5. The family didn't have much money in "the 1980s." ____
6. The family were together more often in "the 1980s." ____

4 Find the affirmative form of the sentences in the text.
1. Blair and Morgan didn't want to change the situation.
2. They didn't stop using cell phones.
3. They didn't use an old-fashioned camera.
4. The family didn't travel across Canada.
5. The family didn't save a lot of money.
6. They didn't enjoy spending more time together.

simple past: regular verbs and past time expressions   LANGUAGE **8C**

5 A Look at the sentences in exercise 4. What ending do regular simple past affirmative forms have?

B Underline more regular simple past forms in the text. Then read the Grammar box.

> **Grammar** simple past: regular verbs and past time expressions
>
> **Affirmative:**
> They **listened** to cassettes.
> I **loved** playing video games.
>
> **Negative:**
> They **didn't watch** DVDs.
> Blair **didn't use** a computer for work.
>
> **Past time expressions:**
> **last** week, **last** month, **last** year, **last** summer
> a few years **ago**, a week **ago**, two days **ago**, three hours **ago**
> **yesterday** morning, **yesterday** afternoon, **yesterday** evening
>
> **Look!** We say **last night**, NOT **yesterday night**. We can also say **last** evening.

Go to Grammar practice: simple past: regular verbs and past time expressions, page 127

6 A ▶ 8.13 **Pronunciation:** -ed endings Listen and repeat the three verbs in the chart. Notice how we say the -ed endings.

/t/	/d/	/ɪd/
looked	changed	wanted

B ▶ 8.14 Add the verbs in the box to the chart. Listen, check, and repeat.

tried   decided   stopped   traveled   played   watched   waited   liked   ended

7 ▶ 8.15 Say the sentences. Listen, check, and repeat.
1 We traveled all night.
2 I watched a movie last night.
3 The family saved a lot of money.
4 You needed a new cell phone.
5 My father worked on the weekend.
6 I wanted a new computer.

8 A Write true sentences with affirmative or negative simple past verbs.
1 I _____ dinner last night. (cook)
2 I _____ a photo online yesterday. (post)
3 I _____ to the radio this morning. (listen)
4 I _____ two years ago. (move)
5 I _____ German at school. (study)
6 I _____ in a different city when I was younger. (live)

B In pairs, compare your sentences. Add more information.

A *I cooked dinner last night. I cooked lasagna.*   B *I cooked chicken last night.*

Go to Communication practice: Student A page 163, Student B page 172

9 A Write one thing for each point below.
• A TV program or movie you watched last week: _____
• A place you traveled to last year: _____
• A game or sport that you played last month: _____
• The job that you wanted to do when you were a child: _____

B Work with your classmates. Find someone with the same answer as you.

A *When I was a child, I wanted to be a vet. How about you?*
B *I didn't want to be a vet. I wanted to be a farmer.*

10 Tell your classmates about different people in your class.

Erica wanted to be a farmer when she was a child.

Personal Best   Choose ten years of your life. Write one important thing that happened in each year.   71

8 SKILLS   WRITING   planning and making notes ■ sequencers

8D What happened to you?

1 Think of something interesting that happened to you last week, last month, or last year. Tell your partner.

2 Read Tony's story. Did he get the job?

My nightmare job interview

Last week, I had a job interview. The interview was on Friday at 9:30 a.m. in New York City. On Thursday evening, I prepared a presentation on my laptop and checked the train times and the address of the company. Before the interview, I felt confident. I went to bed early because I wanted to sleep well.

On Friday morning, the problems started. First, I didn't hear my alarm, and I woke up late. I didn't have time to take a shower or have breakfast. I ran out of the house.

It started to rain, so I stopped to buy an umbrella. Then I ran to the station, but I missed my train!

I felt quite stressed, but there was another train in twenty minutes. I called the company, and they changed the interview to 10:30 a.m. I felt a bit more relaxed. Later, I arrived in New York, and I checked my phone to see where the company was. But my phone had no battery! I was very late when I arrived at their office.

After I got to the interview room, I opened my bag to take out my laptop, but it wasn't there! I felt really stressed, and I had a terrible interview. I wasn't surprised when I didn't get the job!

by Tony Smart

3 Read the story again. Order events a–h from 1–8.
   a ☐ The interview started.
   b ☐ Tony checked the address.
   c ☐ They changed the interview time.
   d ☐ He checked the train times.
   e ☐ His phone didn't have any battery.
   f ☐ It started to rain.
   g ☐ He went to the station.
   h ☐ He saw that he didn't have his computer.

🔧 Skill   planning and making notes

Before you write a story about yourself, ask yourself the following questions and make notes:
1 When did it happen?
2 Where were you at the start?
3 What were the main events?
4 How did you feel at different times?
5 What happened in the end?

4 Read the Skill box. Imagine you are Tony and answer the questions in the Skill box.

planning and making notes ■ sequencers   **WRITING**   **SKILLS**   **8D**

5 Match the notes with the different questions in the Skill box.

a fell asleep on the bus to the airport, didn't get off the bus at the airport, missed the plane, slept at the airport
b last month
c London, on vacation
d got a flight the next day
e tired (on the bus), stressed and angry (at the airport), very tired, but happy (the next day)

Text builder | sequencers

We can connect events with words such as *first*, *then*, *later*, *before*, and *after*. We use these to show the time order of the events:
First, I got up late. Then I took a shower. Later, I went out for coffee.

We use *before* and *after* + a noun or verb phrase:
Before the interview, …
After I got to the interview room, …

6 Read the Text builder. <u>Underline</u> the sequencers in the story on page 72.

7 Choose the correct sequencers to complete the sentences.
1 I always walk my dog in the evening *before / after* I go to bed.
2 *First / Before*, I had a cup of coffee. Then I went shopping.
3 I felt very tired on the trip home. *Later / Before*, I fell asleep on the sofa.
4 We bought some food. *First / Then* we made a nice meal.
5 Are you coming before or *after / later* dinner?

8 Complete the text with the words in the box.

then   first   later   before   after (x2)

I had a terrible day yesterday. ¹_____, the coffee machine broke – I always have a cup of coffee ²_____ I leave the house. ³_____ I couldn't find my car keys. ⁴_____ 30 minutes, I found them in my jacket pocket. ⁵_____, I had an argument with a colleague at work. It was awful, so I went to speak to my boss. ⁶_____ I spoke to her about the situation, I felt a lot better.

9 Write sentences about yesterday. Use the sequencers in exercise 8.
After I arrived at work, I made a large cup of coffee.

10 A **PREPARE** Think about a good/bad/strange experience you had. Make notes about these things:
• the introduction to the story: When did it happen? Where were you? Who were you with?
• the events of the story: What happened? What problems did you have? What did you do? How did you feel? What happened in the end?

B **PRACTICE** Write a story about your experience.

C **PERSONAL BEST** Read another student's story. Check that:
• the introduction is clear.
• the events of the story are clear.
• the verbs are in the correct simple past form.
• the sequencers show the order of events clearly.

Personal Best Choose a well-known movie and describe the events. Ask your partner to guess the movie.   73

7 and 8 REVIEW and PRACTICE

Grammar

1 Choose the correct options to complete the sentences.

1 How _____ fruit do you eat in a week?
 a many
 b often
 c much

2 I have _____ eggs every day for breakfast.
 a an
 b any
 c two

3 There isn't _____ milk in the fridge.
 a any
 b some
 c a

4 For this recipe, I need some peas and _____ .
 a any onions
 b some onions
 c a onion

5 How _____ are there for dinner?
 a much people
 b many people
 c many persons

6 There isn't _____ cheese.
 a lot of
 b a lot of
 c a lot

7 Last night, there _____ any bread in the store.
 a weren't
 b isn't
 c wasn't

8 My nephew doesn't like _____ green vegetables.
 a a
 b much
 c any

2 Rewrite the sentences with the simple past tense.

1 I sometimes work from home.
 Last Tuesday, I _____ .

2 He often goes to Paris.
 Three weeks ago, he _____ .

3 She often eats out.
 Last night, she _____ .

4 They sometimes play tennis.
 Last weekend, they _____ .

5 I get up early.
 Yesterday morning, I _____ .

6 We visit friends most weekends.
 Last weekend, we _____ .

7 I call my sister most days.
 This morning, I _____ .

8 They see their parents every month.
 Last month, they _____ .

3 Complete the text with the correct form of the verbs in parentheses.

The Brazilian Girl from Silicon Valley

Bel Pesce is a famous Brazilian entrepreneur. When she ¹_____ (be) seventeen she ²_____ (read) about the American university MIT and decided that she ³_____ (want) to study there. She ⁴_____ (find) the name of the only Brazilian graduate from the school and arranged to meet him. She ⁵_____ (take) a box of awards with her and ⁶_____ (spend) hours discussing her ideas with him. After that, she ⁷_____ (decide) to apply to MIT and, three months later, they ⁸_____ (accept) her. She completed her studies and then ⁹_____ (work) for Microsoft, Google, and other IT companies. She ¹⁰_____ (write) a book in 2013 called *The Brazilian Girl from Silicon Valley*.

Vocabulary

1 Circle the word that is different. Explain your answer.

1 apple	juice	pear	banana
2 slice	bottle	jar	box
3 fridge	microwave	GPS	dishwasher
4 cheese	beef	ice cream	milk
5 crackers	beans	carrots	peas
6 coffee	tea	cake	water
7 salad	cereal	pasta	rice
8 tablet	smartphone	freezer	laptop

REVIEW and PRACTICE 7 and 8

2 Match definitions 1–8 with objects a–h.
This is something for:

1 cooking something quickly
2 talking to your friends
3 keeping food frozen
4 taking photos
5 helping you find your way
6 doing the dishes
7 watching TV shows you missed
8 keeping things cold

a digital camera
b freezer
c dishwasher
d GPS
e microwave
f smartphone
g fridge
h video recorder

3 Complete the sentences with the correct form of the verbs in the box.

meet   finish   get   have   go   be born   start   retire

1 All of our children _____ in July.
2 My daughter _____ school when she was four years old.
3 You normally can't _____ school before you are sixteen.
4 In the UK, students usually don't live at home when they _____ to college.
5 To get a good job, you need to _____ a good degree.
6 People often _____ their partners at work.
7 My sister _____ her second baby last year.
8 My parents _____ in 2010 at the age of 60.

4 Put the words in the correct columns.

cereal   onions   freezer   carton   fridge
rice   carrots   pepper   dishwasher   bread
bag   glass   cabbage   microwave   pasta

Vegetables	Containers	Kitchen equipment	Grains

Personal Best

Lesson 7A Name five vegetables.

Lesson 8A Name five kitchen objects.

Lesson 7A Think of three kinds of food that are uncountable.

Lesson 8A Write a sentence with *there weren't*.

Lesson 7B Name two pronouns and two possessive adjectives.

Lesson 8B Name six important life stages.

Lesson 7C Write two questions, one with *How much …?* and one with *How many …?*

Lesson 8C Write two sentences beginning *a few years ago*.

Lesson 7C Write a sentence with *a few*.

Lesson 8C List six regular verbs and put them in the simple past.

Lesson 7D Give three phrases for ordering food in a restaurant.

Lesson 8D Write three things you did yesterday with *first*, *then*, and *later*.

75

UNIT 9 Education, education!

LANGUAGE past of *be* and simple past: questions ■ school subjects and education

9A School days

1 Do you have these types of schools in your country? In pairs, discuss the ages when you start and finish each type of school.

We start nursery school when we're two and finish when we're four.

- nursery school
- kindergarten
- preschool
- elementary school (primary school)
- middle school
- high school (secondary school)

2 A Read the text. Do South Korean students study more or less than students in your country?

B Read the text again and answer the questions.

1 What is a *Hagwon*?
2 What do South Korean high school students say you can do if you sleep for three hours?
3 What do they say you can do if you sleep for six hours?
4 What lessons do elementary school students have?
5 What is *Hanja*?

3 Find five school subjects in the text.

School system in South Korea

Education is very important in South Korea. School days are long – students are often in school for eight hours. A lot of parents also send their students to a *Hagwon*, a private school where they have extra lessons before or after their normal school. Teachers give a lot of homework, too. All these hours, weeks, and years of study decide if students do well on their exams and can go to a good college, which is very important in South Korean society. High school students in their last year have a saying: sleep three hours and go to a top college. Sleep six hours and forget about college.

 Nursery school and kindergarten (ages 0–6)
Students can start going to school from a very young age. Playing games is an important part of lessons.

 Elementary school (ages 6–12)
As well as subjects like geography and math, students have lessons about how to be practical, how to enjoy life, and how to have good morals.

 Middle school (ages 12–15)
At this age, students start learning to write *Hanja*, the Chinese characters that are used in the Korean language.

 High school (ages 15–18)
There are different types of high schools, for example, science high schools, foreign language high schools, and art high schools.

Go to Vocabulary practice: school subjects and education, page 151

4 A ▶ 9.3 Listen to Ji-hoon. Are the sentences true (T) or false (F)?

1 He started nursery school when he was two years old. ____
2 He went to a *Hagwon* in middle school. ____
3 He was good at English. ____
4 He went to an arts high school. ____
5 He went to the library after school. ____
6 He didn't go to college. ____

past of *be* and simple past: questions ■ school subjects and education   LANGUAGE 9A

B ▶ 9.3 Listen again and complete the questions.
1 When _____ you _____ school?
2 _____ you _____ school?
3 What _____ your best subject?
4 _____ you good at English?
5 _____ you _____ a lot of homework?
6 _____ you _____ into college?

5 Look at the questions in 4B and complete the rules. Then read the Grammar box.
1 For the verb *be*, we make past questions with (question word) + _____ / _____ + subject.
2 For other verbs, we make past questions with (question word) + _____ + subject + infinitive.

Grammar — past: questions

Past of *be*:
Were you a good student?
Was English your favorite subject?
Who *was* your teacher?
What *were* your worst subjects?

Simple past:
Did you *enjoy* school?
Did your school *have* a swimming pool?
What subjects *did* you *study* in high school?
Where *did* you *go* to college?

Go to Grammar practice: past: questions, page 128

6 A ▶ 9.5 **Pronunciation:** intonation in questions Listen to the questions. Do they have rising ↗ or falling ↘ intonation at the end?
1 Did you enjoy school?
2 Were you a good student?
3 Did you study music in school?
4 Where did you go to college?
5 What was your favorite subject?
6 Why did you study Russian?

B Match the beginnings of rules a–b with the endings.
a ↗ We use rising intonation for …   questions with a question word.
b ↘ We use falling intonation for …   questions with a *yes/no* answer.

7 ▶ 9.5 Say the questions from 6A. Listen, check, and repeat.

8 Complete the questions with *did*, *was*, or *were*. Then ask and answer the questions in pairs.
1 What subjects _____ you study in high school?
2 What _____ your favorite subject?
3 _____ there a lot of homework?
4 What subjects _____ you good and bad at?
5 When _____ you start and finish high school?
6 _____ you do well on your exams in school?

Go to Communication practice: Student A page 164, Student B page 173

9 A Look at the sentences. Decide what questions you need to ask.
1 Did you do homework before school?

Find a classmate who …	Name:
1 did homework before school.	_____
2 studied until ten in the evening.	_____
3 was the best student in his/her class in school.	_____
4 had classes on Saturdays.	_____
5 was very good at math.	_____
6 played sports for his/her school.	_____
7 learned a musical instrument in school.	_____
8 didn't enjoy school.	_____

B Ask different classmates the questions. Try to find someone different for each sentence. Give more information when you answer the questions.
A *Did you play sports for your school?*   B *Yes, I did. I was on the school basketball team!*

Personal Best Find someone who went to school in another town or city. Ask him/her five questions about his/her school.

9 SKILLS READING understanding words that you don't know ■ *because* and *so*

9B Lifelong learning

1 A Look at the skills. Check (✓) the ones that you can do now. Cross out (X) the ones that you can't do.
- drive a car
- ride a bike
- speak German
- play a musical instrument
- sail a boat
- create a website

B Discuss how you learned to do each skill in pairs.

I took driving lessons when I was eighteen.

2 Read the introduction to each section in the text. Match the headings with the sections.

Adult learning   Homeschooling   Self-study

3 Work in groups of three. Each person reads one of the interviews. Close your books and tell your group about the person in the interview.

I read about Ana. Her parents homeschooled her because …

Skill — understanding words that you don't know

When you read a text, don't worry if there are words you don't understand. First, read the whole text to understand the main idea. Then look at the new words. Ask yourself these questions:
- Are they verbs, nouns, or adjectives?
- Do they look similar to words in your language?
- Does the topic or sentence help you understand the meaning?

4 A Read the Skill box and look at the sentences from the text. Are the **bold** words verbs, nouns, or adjectives?
1. Some of the world's most **successful** people had parents who chose homeschooling. _____
2. I didn't enjoy it at first because I **missed** my friends. _____
3. He **cofounded** WhatsApp, the world's most popular messaging app, with Brian Acton. _____
4. Do you have any **advice** for people who want to teach themselves something? _____

B In pairs, discuss what you think the words mean. Use the text to help you. Check in a dictionary to see if you are right.

Text builder — *because* and *so*

We use *because* to give a reason:
I didn't enjoy it at first because I missed my friends.

We use *so* to give a result:
The lessons were really easy for me, so my parents decided to teach me at home.

5 A Read the Text builder. Underline more reasons and results with *because* and *so* in the text.

B Match the two parts of the sentences and include *because* or *so* to complete them.
1. I found math difficult
2. My grandfather is getting a part-time degree
3. There are lots of self-study videos online
4. I wanted to be a lawyer when I was younger
5. I wanted to homeschool my children

a. I wanted to earn a lot of money!
b. he didn't go to college when he was younger.
c. I went to night school to take extra classes.
d. I left my job to teach them.
e. it's really easy to learn a new skill.

6 Discuss the questions about homeschooling, self-study, and adult learning in pairs.
1. What are the good and bad things about homeschooling?
2. Are you learning something by yourself right now, or would you like to? What activity or subject is it?
3. Would you like to go back to school when you're older? Why/Why not?

78

understanding words that you don't know ■ *because* and *so*   READING   SKILLS   9B

DIFFERENT PATHS →

Ana, 25, researcher

1 _____

In the U.S., about 2.5 million young people have their classes at home. Some of the world's most successful people had parents who homeschooled them: the scientist Michael Faraday, the rock group the Jonas Brothers, and Soichiro Honda, who started Honda cars.

Ana, why did you have classes at home?
In elementary school, classes were really easy for me – I helped the teacher! So my parents decided to teach me at home.

Did your mother or father teach you?
My mother taught me math and science, and my father taught me geography, history, and politics.

Did you like learning at home?
I didn't enjoy it at first because I missed my friends. But I really enjoyed studying with my two brothers.

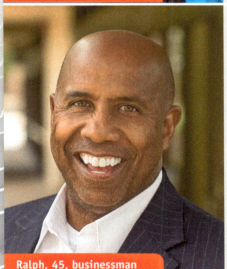

Ralph, 45, businessman

2 _____

A lot of successful people learn their skills themselves. David Karp, who started the photo blog website Tumblr, taught himself to program. Jan Koum is another programmer who learned through self-study. He cofounded WhatsApp, the world's most popular messaging app, with Brian Acton.

Ralph, why did you become interested in programming?
I loved making things and solving puzzles when I was a child. With programming, you can do both.

Did you learn programming in school?
No! I went to school in the 1980s. They only had one computer in the whole school, so I taught myself to program from books.

Do you have any advice for people who want to teach themselves something?
It can be hard without a teacher, so you need to love the subject that you're learning.

Eva, 73, retired secretary

3 _____

A lot of people go back to school later in life. In 2007, singer Shakira took a college course on the history of western civilization. Basketball star Shaquille O'Neal left college to play in the NBA. He went back to school in 2000, and by 2012, he was Dr. O'Neal. Next on his list? Law school.

Eva, when did you leave school?
I left school at 16. I got married and had four children. I worked part time.

Why did you start to study again?
I started going to night school because I wanted to learn a foreign language. I chose French.

When did you go to college?
When I retired, I went to college to study French. I graduated when I was 73!

Personal Best Describe what type of student you are. Do you find learning new things easy?   79

9 LANGUAGE verb patterns: verb + infinitive ■ resolutions

9C Change your life

1 A Read the introduction to the text. Did you make a New Year's resolution this year? Did you keep it? Discuss in pairs.

B Complete the text with the phrases in the box.

> get in shape   save money   improve your diet   get a new job   be more organized

Apps
TO CHANGE YOUR LIFE

On January 1st every year, millions of us make New Year's resolutions – things that we want to change in our lives.

But only 8% of us are successful! Here are some top apps that can help you keep your resolutions.

MYWELLNESS
This app encourages you to ¹_____. If you join a gym and scan the code on the machines, it records all the exercise that you get. It also helps you plan your exercise goals.

ALLRECIPES
You can get bored eating the same food every day. You tell Allrecipes what's in your cabinets and fridge, and it gives you some new and healthy recipes. It's a great way to ²_____.

TOSHL FINANCE
This app teaches people to ³_____. It shows you how you spend your money and gives you ideas about how to save.

EVERNOTE
This is a great planning app for students who want to ⁴_____. It organizes your study plans and gives you to-do lists. It can help you get good grades and pass exams.

SWITCH
This app can encourage you to ⁵_____. If you see a job you like, you can contact the company. They see your profile but not your name, so you can keep it a secret from your manager!

2 In pairs, look at the apps again. Tell your partner which apps you think are good for you and why.

I think Allrecipes is a good app for me. I usually eat the same food every day.

Go to Vocabulary practice: resolutions, page 152

3 A ▶9.7 Listen to people talking about the changes they want to make. Match the people with the apps from the text.

1 Megan _____   3 Tatyana _____   5 Raymond _____
2 Zafar _____   4 María _____

B ▶9.7 Listen again. Complete the sentences with the verbs in the box.

> need (x2)   'm planning   want   'd like   hope

1 I _____ to learn how to cook some new things.
2 I _____ to save money for my vacation.
3 I _____ to get a new job this year.
4 I _____ to lose six kilos before the summer.
5 I _____ to go to college next year, so I _____ to get good grades and pass my exams.

verb patterns: verb + infinitive ■ resolutions   LANGUAGE **9C**

4 Complete the rule. Then read the Grammar box.

After verbs like *want*, *need*, *hope*, and *plan*, we can use an _____.

> 📖 **Grammar** | verb patterns: verb + infinitive
>
> I **want to improve** my diet.   I'm **planning to save** more money this year.
> I **need to get** more exercise every week.   I'**d like to get** a new job.
>
> **Look!** *'d like* is the contracted form of **would like**. It means **want**, not **like**.
> I '**d like to** join a gym this year. BUT I **like** going to the gym.

Go to Grammar practice: verb patterns: verb + infinitive, page 129

5 A ▶9.9 **Pronunciation:** *'d like* and *like* Listen and repeat.

I'd like	I would like	I like
you'd like	you would like	you like
we'd like	we would like	we like

B ▶9.10 Say the sentences. Listen, check, and repeat.

1 I'd like to speak French.
2 I like speaking French.
3 We'd like to play more sports.
4 We like playing sports.
5 They'd like to go on vacation.
6 They like going on vacation.

6 A Match the two parts to make complete sentences. Some items have more than one possible answer.

1 I didn't get any exercise last week. I need
2 I want to get a job in another country, so I need
3 I'm living in a new city. I hope
4 I have a test next week. I'm planning
5 I have a lot of free time. I'd like
6 I want to get a better job, but I need

a to make some new friends.
b to start a new hobby.
c to improve my English.
d to go to the gym this week.
e to improve my skills.
f to study every evening.

B Which of the sentences are true for you? Tell your partner.

I need to improve my English because I want to work in Canada one day.

Go to Communication practice: Student A page 164, Student B page 173

7 A Think of one idea for each option. Write your answers in the shapes.

- a person that you're planning to visit next week
- a place where you hope to go on vacation one day
- a language that you'd like to learn
- a person that you want to speak to today
- a place where you'd like to live one day
- something that you're planning to buy this year

B Show your partner your answers. Ask each other questions about them and explain why you wrote them.

A *Why did you write "Barcelona"?*
B *Because I'd like to live in Barcelona one day. I think it's a really cool city.*

Personal Best Plan a new app to help people change their lives. What does your app do? Think of a name for it.

9 SKILLS SPEAKING making suggestions ■ sounding sympathetic

9D What's the problem?

1 A Match problems 1–5 with pictures a–e.

1 I'm stressed at work. ___
2 I'm always tired. ___
3 I'm homesick, and I miss my family. ___
4 My exams aren't going well. ___
5 I'm having problems with my boyfriend/girlfriend. ___

B Do you sometimes have these problems? Discuss in pairs.

I don't sleep well, and I'm always tired.

2 ▶ 9.11 Watch or listen to the first part of *Learning Curve*. What's Marc's problem? Choose the correct option.

a He didn't finish his final exam.
b He arrived late for his exam.
c He thinks he failed his exam.

3 ▶ 9.11 Watch or listen again. Are the sentences true (T) or false (F)?

1 Marc studied hard for this exam. ___
2 He has two jobs. ___
3 He's stressed, and he's always tired. ___
4 His sister sent him some candy for good luck. ___

4 A Look at Penny's text message to Marc. What two suggestions does she make? How does Marc respond?

> Hi Marc! I know you're stressed at the moment. Why don't you take a break from studying? How about meeting me and Ethan for coffee? We're waiting for you at the café. Penny

> That's a really good idea. Thanks, Penny! I'm on my way.

B Complete the sentences to make two more suggestions for Marc.

1 Why don't you …
2 How about …

Conversation builder | making suggestions

Making suggestions:
Why don't you talk with your family now?
What/How about visit**ing** your parents later this month?
Can you take some time off work?
Let's do something quiet tonight.

Responding to suggestions:
I'm not sure I should.
That's a (really) good idea.

making suggestions ■ sounding sympathetic   **SPEAKING**   SKILLS   **9D**

5 Read the Conversation builder. In pairs, make suggestions for the problems in Exercise 1, and respond.

6 ▶ 9.12 Watch or listen to the second part of the show. Which problem from exercise 1 does Penny have? What two suggestions does Ethan make?

7 ▶ 9.12 Watch or listen again and complete the extracts with the words in the box.

awful   sorry   shame   no

Penny	My parents can't come to New York on holiday until next spring.
Ethan	Oh, I'm ¹_____ to hear that.
...	
Penny	I'm homesick!
Ethan	Oh ²_____! Poor you!
...	
Marc	I couldn't remember the answer to one of the math problems. I was too tired.
Penny	That's a ³_____.
...	
Marc	I was so tired I fell asleep on the train. I almost missed my exam!
Penny	How ⁴_____!

> **Skill** sounding sympathetic
>
> If someone has bad news or feels unhappy, we can show that we are sympathetic.
>
> • Use falling intonation: *That's a shame!*   *How terrible!*   *Poor you!*
> • Say you're sorry to hear his/her news: *Oh no! I'm sorry to hear that.*
> • Show you understand that the situation is bad/difficult: *I'm sure it's difficult to (be so far away from your family).*

8 A ▶ 9.13 Read the Skill box. Listen and repeat the expressions of sympathy when you hear the beeps.

B In pairs, take turns saying sentences 1–6 and respond with sympathy. Use intonation to sound sympathetic.
1 I don't sleep well because my neighbors are very noisy.
2 I can never find the time to study because I have two jobs.
3 My girlfriend/boyfriend isn't speaking to me.
4 I missed my nine o'clock class again, and the teacher wants to speak to me.
5 I have a $2,000 credit card bill!
6 I didn't get into college last year.

Go to Communication practice: Student A page 164, Student B page 173

9 A PREPARE Think of three problems you sometimes have or had in the past. Use the following ideas and your own ideas.
• problems at work/with education
• problems with your family or partner
• problems with your friends
• problems with money

B PRACTICE In pairs, take turns describing your problems. Show sympathy, make suggestions, and respond to the suggestions. Use a variety of phrases.

C PERSONAL BEST Repeat the activity with a different partner. Did they use different phrases from the Conversation builder? Did they sound sympathetic? Who made the best suggestions?

Personal Best   Write a short conversation between two friends about a problem one of them has.   83

UNIT 10 People

LANGUAGE   comparative adjectives ■ adjectives to describe places

10A First dates

1 A Make pairs of opposite adjectives. Use them to describe the places in the pictures.

empty   unfriendly   safe   light   crowded   friendly   dark   dangerous

a    b    c    d    e

B Use the adjectives to talk about places in your town or city.

The subway is always really crowded.

The downtown area is safe during the day, but it can be dangerous at night.

Go to Vocabulary practice: adjectives to describe places, page 152

2 Read the definition of a first date. Choose three good places for a first date from the ideas below. Discuss in pairs.

first date: a meeting, usually at a restaurant, movie theater, etc., with a new person when you're looking for a boyfriend or girlfriend

a restaurant   a movie theater   a café   your house   a shopping mall   a club   a bowling alley

3 Read the text. Which three places are a bad idea for a first date? Which three places are a good idea?

Where NOT to go on a first date

You have a date with someone special, and you don't know where to go. Don't make the mistake of choosing the wrong place. **Here are three places not to go!**

1 A movie theater
Do you want to sit in a dark room in silence during your first date? No? Then don't go to the movies! How about going to the park instead? Nothing is more important than conversation on a first date, and a walk in the park gives you lots of time to talk and have fun together. It's more romantic than a movie theater, and it's also cheaper. In fact, it's free!

2 A club
Music, dancing, beautiful people … a date at a club sounds great! Or maybe not. It's impossible to talk, and a lot of people don't feel comfortable on a crowded dance floor. Why not go bowling? A bowling alley is quieter and more relaxed than a club, and it's cheaper!

3 An expensive restaurant
It's a popular first date, but a meal in an expensive restaurant is often a bad idea. It can be hard to relax and be yourself in a restaurant, especially if it's pretty quiet. It's better to meet in a café for a cup of coffee or lunch. It's more comfortable than a restaurant, and if things aren't going well, it's also easier to escape!

Our final piece of advice: don't be late. There's nothing worse than a late date!

comparative adjectives ■ adjectives to describe places   LANGUAGE **10A**

4 Complete the sentences with words from the text.
1 It's _____ than a movie theater.
2 A bowling alley is _____ and _____ than a club.
3 It's _____ to meet in a café.
4 It's also _____ to escape!
5 There's nothing _____ than a late date!

5 Look at the sentences in exercise 4 and complete the grammar rules. Then read the Grammar box.
1 To make the comparative form of a short adjective, for example, *cheap*, we add _____.
2 To make the comparative form of a long adjective, for example, *comfortable*, we put _____ before it.
3 The comparative forms of *good* and *bad* are _____ and _____.

Grammar comparative adjectives

Short adjectives (one syllable or two syllables ending -y):
It's **cheaper** than a movie theater.
It's **harder** to relax in a restaurant.
It's **easier** to escape.

Long adjectives:
Nothing is **more important** than conversation.
A bowling alley is **more relaxed** than a club.

Irregular adjectives:
A café is **better** than a restaurant.
A date in a movie theater is **worse** than in a park.

Go to Grammar practice: comparative adjectives, page 130

6 A ▶10.3 **Pronunciation:** *-er* endings Listen and repeat the adjectives and comparatives.
big – bigger   noisy – noisier   cheap – cheaper   empty – emptier

B ▶10.4 Say the sentences. Listen, check, and repeat.
1 Bangkok is cheaper than Singapore.
2 Tokyo is safer than Los Angeles.
3 Winters are darker in Iceland than in Sweden.
4 Zurich is quieter than Rome.
5 The market is friendlier than the shopping center.
6 The bus is busier than the train.

7 A ▶10.5 George and Lola are discussing restaurants for a first date. Match the adjectives with each restaurant. Listen and check.

cheap   crowded   expensive   good (food)
quiet   romantic   relaxed

B Compare Mimi's and Luigi's in pairs.
Mimi's is more romantic than Luigi's.

Mimi's

Luigi's

Communication practice: Student A page 165, Student B page 174

8 In pairs, think of places in your town or city. Discuss where to go and what to do for the special occasions below.
A *I think Pizza Palace is a good place for a second date.*
B *I'm not sure. I think a café like Coffee House is better because you can relax there.*

a second date   a friend's 30th birthday   your grandmother's birthday
your niece's second birthday   a big family get-together
a school reunion   other ideas

Personal Best Write ten comparative sentences about cities in your country.   85

10 SKILLS LISTENING listening for detailed information (1) ■ weak forms ■ describing appearance

10B You look so different!

1 Match the words in the box with pictures a–c.

straight hair   beard   red hair   glasses   curly hair   elderly   middle-aged   blond hair   bald   young

Go to Vocabulary practice: describing appearance, page 153

2 In pairs, think of people you know and describe their appearance.

A *My father has a beard.*   B *My friend Amanda has blond hair. She's tall and slim.*

3 ▶ 10.7 Watch or listen to the first part of *Learning Curve*. Choose the correct definition of "disguise."

a A disguise is something that helps you look younger.
b A disguise is something that changes the color of your hair.
c A disguise is something that makes you look like a different person.

Skill listening for detailed information (1)

It is often necessary to understand what someone says in detail.
- Read the questions before you listen and think about the possible answers.
- Listen for words that introduce the information that you need. For example, if you need the name of a movie, listen for the word "film" or "movie."
- Wait until the speaker has finished speaking before you answer the question.

4 A ▶ 10.7 Read the Skill box and questions 1–6 below. Watch or listen again. Complete the sentences.

1 Ethan mentions a movie called *The Master of _____*.
2 In the movie, the actor Dana Carvey becomes an overweight, _____ character.
3 In another scene, Dana is a middle-aged woman with _____ hair.
4 Dark lines on an actor's face can make him or her look _____.
5 Lucia Pittalis can make her eyes look smaller or her lips look _____.
6 A wig can make your hair look _____ or _____.

B Do you know any movies where someone has a disguise? Tell your partner about the movie.

listening for detailed information (1) ■ weak forms ■ describing appearance **LISTENING** SKILLS **10 B**

5 ▶ 10.8 Watch or listen to the second part of the show. Match the things that the people change in their makeovers with the names below. You can use one word more than once.

beard   eyes   hair   mustache

1 Ginny _____   2 Ron _____   3 Malika _____

6 ▶ 10.8 Watch or listen again. Are the sentences true (T) or false (F)?
1 Ginny wants straight hair. ____
2 She wants her lips to look bigger. ____
3 Ron wants a makeover because he has a new job. ____
4 After his makeover, he feels lighter. ____
5 Malika usually has long, curly hair. ____
6 Malika thinks she looks taller after her makeover. ____
7 Her boyfriend talked a lot when he saw her. ____
8 Ginny thinks she looks younger after her makeover. ____

7 Discuss the questions in pairs.
1 How important is your appearance to you? (1 = not important, 10 = very important)
2 How much time and money do you spend on your appearance each week?
3 Do you want to look different? If so, what do you want to change?

Listening builder   **weak forms**

In English, we don't usually stress words like articles and prepositions. These words sound shorter and weaker than important words like nouns, verbs, and adjectives:
One of the best makeup artists in the world is Kevin Yagher.
I have an interview for a new job later, in an art gallery.

8 A Read the Listening builder. Read the sentences and underline the words which you think have weak forms.
1 The people in the movie were very young.
2 His character was an elderly man with a long white beard.
3 She puts a lot of makeup on their faces.
4 I like your hair. I think the color looks great.
5 The name of her character was Emma.
6 My brother has a long beard and a mustache.

B ▶ 10.9 Listen and check.

9 A Look at the photos of two makeovers. In pairs, describe the photos from "before" and "after" the makeovers.

B In pairs, answer the questions.
1 How does the man/woman look different now?
2 Do they look better or worse after their makeovers in your opinion? Why?

Personal Best   Imagine you had a makeover. Describe your new appearance.

10 LANGUAGE — superlative adjectives ■ personality adjectives

10C The yearbook

1 Look at the adjectives in the box. Think of someone you know for each one. Tell your partner.

> smart   lazy   shy   polite   popular   kind   funny

My nephew is very smart. He's studying math in college.

Go to Vocabulary practice: personality adjectives, page 154

2 A Look at the pictures. Which famous person can you see? Read the text quickly. Which other famous people does it mention and why?

B Read the text again. Which of these things can you find in a yearbook? What else does a yearbook include?

- personal stories about people in the school
- exam results
- photos of students
- students' e-mail addresses
- students' plans for the future

3 Match the awards with the celebrities. There are three extra awards.

1 Renée Zellweger
2 Michael Jackson
3 Jack Nicholson

a the worst dancer
b the most beautiful girl
c the nicest personality
d the laziest student
e the shyest classmate
f the best actor

THE YEARBOOK

"The best athlete" … "The nicest personality"… "The worst dancer." Welcome to the yearbook, an important tradition in the U.S. and other countries. A yearbook is like a photo album, with photos of all the students in one year in a high school or college. Students write about sports teams and clubs, they remember funny stories about their classmates and teachers, and they write about their future plans.

A yearbook also includes awards. These can be for the friendliest teacher, the laziest student, the funniest laugh, and so on. In high school, Renée Zellweger was "The most beautiful girl," Jack Nicholson was "The best actor," and Michael Jackson was "The shyest classmate." Here's a surprising one – in his school, "The least likely to be successful" was … Tom Cruise!

Some people say that high school and college are the happiest days of our lives. And, for millions of students, the yearbook is an important way of remembering that time.

4 Look at the adjectives in exercise 3 and answer the questions. Then read the Grammar box.

1 What letters do we add to a short adjective to make the superlative form? _____
2 What word do we use before long adjectives? _____
3 What is the superlative form of *good* and *bad*? _____ and _____
4 What word comes before all superlative forms? _____

superlative adjectives ■ personality adjectives   LANGUAGE **10C**

Grammar superlative adjectives

Short adjectives (one syllable or two syllables ending -y):
She's **the nicest** person in our class.
High school and college are **the happiest** days of our lives.

Long adjectives:
She's **the most popular** girl in the school.
Our teacher is **the most interesting** person that I know.

Irregular adjectives:
He's **the best** dancer in the school.
This is **the worst** photo of me.

Go to Grammar practice: superlative adjectives, page 131

5 A ▶ 10.12 **Pronunciation:** superlative adjectives Listen and repeat the superlatives.

the nicest   the funniest   the most popular   the most relaxed

B ▶ 10.13 Say the sentences. Listen, check, and repeat.
1 You're the kindest person that I know.
2 He's the laziest person in the office.
3 She has the most beautiful voice.
4 It's the most exciting movie of the year.

Go to Communication practice: Student A page 165, Student B page 174

6 Complete the text about Ashrita Furman with the superlative forms of the adjectives in the box.

popular   high   strange   heavy   tall   fast

The **most world records** on the planet

The *Guinness Book of World Records* is one of the ¹_____ books on Earth. If you have a copy, you will probably notice the name Ashrita Furman. This is because Ashrita has ²_____ number of world records on the planet – more than 200! And his records are also some of the ³_____ records in the book. Here are a few:

The ⁴_____ shoes in the world
In November 2010, Ashrita walked around London in shoes that weighed 146.5 kg.

The ⁵_____ object balanced on the nose
In August 2015, Ashrita balanced a 15.95 m. pole on his nose in New York.

The ⁶_____ mile with a milk bottle on the head
In February 2004, in Indonesia, Ashrita ran a mile in 7 minutes, 47 seconds, balancing a milk bottle on his head.

7 A Write sentences that are true for you.

The kindest person that I know is my friend María.

The (kind) person that I know is …
The (old) person in my family is …
The (lazy) person that I know is …
The (funny) person on TV is …
The (good) movie of the year so far is …

The (interesting) show on TV at the moment is …
The (beautiful) place in my country is …
The (expensive) place in my town is …

B Ask and answer questions about your answers to exercise 7A in pairs.

Who's the kindest person that you know?

8 A In groups, create your own class awards. Discuss and choose an award for each student. Use the ideas in the boxes and your own ideas.

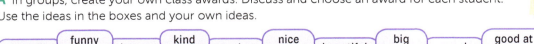

friendly   funny   happy   kind   good at English   nice laugh   beautiful hair   big smile   good clothes   good at sports

I think Eduardo always wears really cool clothes. Let's give him an award for the best clothes.

B Share your awards with the class.

We'd like to give Elena the award for "the friendliest student".

Personal Best Write ten superlative sentences about people and places that you know.

10 SKILLS WRITING writing a description of a person ■ clauses with *when*

10D Someone that I admire

1 Is there someone that you admire? It could be a friend, a family member, or someone famous. Why do you admire him or her? Discuss in pairs.

I admire my aunt. She's a surgeon, and she saves people's lives. It's a really difficult and important job.

2 A Read Hannah's description. Who does she admire and why?

B Read the description again and answer the questions.
1. What does Michaela look like?
2. What happened when she was three years old?
3. When did she move to the Dutch National Ballet?
4. Who does Michaela help?
5. What difficult situation did Hannah have?

A PERSON I ADMIRE
Michaela DePrince

Michaela DePrince is a ballet dancer from Sierra Leone. She's unusual in the world of ballet because there aren't many ballerinas from her country. She is slim and confident and has a beautiful smile. ¹_____

From a young age, Michaela's life was extremely difficult. When she was three years old, she lost both her parents in the civil war in Sierra Leone. But she survived her difficult past, and today she's one of the most talented young ballet stars in the world. She became the youngest dancer at the Dance Theatre of Harlem in New York when she was just seventeen and, in 2013, she moved to the Dutch National Ballet. ²_____

I admire Michaela because she's a very strong and brave person. As well as ballet dancing, she spends a lot of time helping young people who have problems in their lives. ³_____ When I didn't get the grades that I needed to study medicine in college, Michaela's story inspired me, and I didn't give up.

By Hannah Lee

 Skill writing a description of a person

When you write a description of a person, organize your ideas into paragraphs, for example:
Paragraph 1: where the person is from, his/her job, appearance, and personality
Ed Sheeran is a singer and musician from England. He has red hair and blue eyes, and is very popular.

Paragraph 2: information about his/her life and achievements
He was born in 1991 in Yorkshire. When he was a child, he learned to play the guitar. He made his first record when he was thirteen. Today, he is popular all over the world.

Paragraph 3: why you admire him/her
I admire him because he writes beautiful and honest songs, and he's very talented.

3 Read the Skill box. Complete 1–3 in the description of Michaela DePrince with sentences a–c.
a She shows that there is always hope for a better future.
b In 2016, she danced in Beyoncé's visual album, *Lemonade*.
c For a ballerina, she's not very tall.

writing a description of a person ■ clauses with *when*   **WRITING**   **SKILLS**   **10D**

4 Organize the sentences about Lionel Messi into three paragraphs.

a He played his first game for Barcelona when he was seventeen and quickly became one of their most important players.
b When Lionel was a young boy, he began playing soccer. FC Barcelona soon noticed him and, when he was thirteen, he moved to Spain.
c He's 1.7 m. tall and has dark brown hair.
d Lionel Messi is not only a fantastic soccer player, but he's also a great person.
e He's generous and kind, and he does a lot to help children's charities.
f Lionel Messi is a soccer player from Argentina. He plays for FC Barcelona in Spain and for his national team, Argentina.

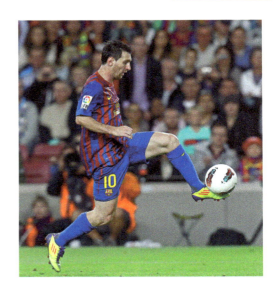

Text builder — clauses with *when*

We use a clause with *when* to talk about two things that happened in the past:
When she was three years old, she lost both her parents.
She became the youngest dancer at the Dance Theatre of Harlem when she was just seventeen.

We use the clause with *when* for the action that happened or started first:
When she arrived in the U.S., she joined the Dance Theatre of Harlem.

5 A Read the Text builder. Choose the correct option to complete the rules.
1 When a clause with *when* comes before the main clause, we *use / don't use* a comma.
2 When a clause with *when* comes after the main clause, we *use / don't use* a comma.

B Join the two sentences with a clause with *when*. Write two versions for each sentence.

He was eighteen. At that time, he moved to Australia.

When he was eighteen, he moved to Australia.
He moved to Australia when he was eighteen.

1 She finished college. After that, she became a photographer.
2 His mother died. After that, he went to live with his aunt.
3 I was a student. At that time, I met my wife.
4 I had a problem at work. That's when my best friend gave me some good advice.
5 She was thirty. At that time, she had her first baby.
6 He retired. He learned to play the guitar.

6 A PREPARE Make notes about a person that you admire. Think about these questions:
• What does he/she do? What does he/she look like? What is he/she like?
• What do you know about his/her life and achievements?
• Why do you admire him/her?

B PRACTICE Write a description. Use the heading *A person that I admire*.

Paragraph 1: Describe the person.
Paragraph 2: Describe the most important events of his/her life.
Paragraph 3: Describe why you admire the person.

C PERSONAL BEST Read your partner's description. Correct any mistakes and give suggestions for improvement.

Personal Best Think of a famous person who is unusual in his/her profession. Write some facts about him/her.

9 and 10 REVIEW and PRACTICE

Grammar

1 Cross out (**X**) the sentence that is NOT correct.

1. a Where did you go last weekend? ____
   b Where went you last weekend? ____
   c Where were you last weekend? ____

2. a Were you study English in elementary school? ____
   b Did you study English in elementary school? ____
   c Were you happy in elementary school? ____

3. a He wanted finish the job. ____
   b He agreed to finish the job. ____
   c He decided to finish the job. ____

4. a We're planning to go away this weekend. ____
   b We would like to go away this weekend. ____
   c We need going away this weekend. ____

5. a My sister's older than me. ____
   b I'm younger than her. ____
   c She's more old than me. ____

6. a This question's more easy than the others. ____
   b This question's easier than the others. ____
   c This question's the easiest. ____

7. a This hotel's the most expensive in the town. ____
   b This hotel's the more expensive in the town. ____
   c It's also the most comfortable. ____

8. a Who's the better player in the world? ____
   b Who's the best player in the world? ____
   c Who's the most popular player in the world? ____

2 Make comparative sentences with the adjectives in parentheses.

1. John's 20 and Sophie's 21. (young)
   _____
2. Flight A's $400 and Flight B's $300. (expensive)
   _____
3. The cheetah has a top speed of 95 km. an hour, and the lion about 80 km. an hour. (fast)
   _____
4. A mile's about 1,500 m., and a kilometer is 1,000 m. (long)
   _____
5. A bike's lighter than a car. (heavy)
   _____
6. The Nile's 6,800 km., and the Yangtze's 6,500 km. (short)
   _____
7. My mother's 70. My father's 68. (old)
   _____
8. Player A's number 1 in the world. Player B's number 25. (good)
   _____

3 Complete the questions in the dialogue.

The man who beat Pokémon Go

1. Q Congratulations! H____ l____ d____ i____ t____ y____ ?
   A It took me just over two weeks.
2. Q H____ m____ d____ y____ c____ ?
   A I caught 142.
3. Q W____ d____ y____ f____ t____ ?
   A I found them in New York City.
4. Q H____ m____ d____ y____ s____ ?
   A I spent about $200.
5. Q H____ f____ d____ y____ w____ ?
   A I walked about 200 km.
6. Q So it was a healthy activity. D____ y____ l____ any weight?
   A Yes, I did. I lost about five kilos.
7. Q W____ d____ y____ p____ i____ ?
   A I played it for my work. I work for a tech company in Manhattan.
8. Q W____ y____ a Pokémon fan as a child?
   A Yes, I was. I played it in 1996 on my Game Boy.

Vocabulary

1 Circle the word that is different.

1	chemistry	physics	history	biology
2	take	get into	pass	fail
3	get in shape	get a job	lose weight	get exercise
4	short	slim	empty	tall
5	crowded	dark	dangerous	kind
6	curly	young	gray	straight
7	lazy	nice	polite	brave
8	school	college	gym	kindergarten

92

REVIEW and PRACTICE 9 and 10

Personal Best

2 Match definitions 1–8 with adjectives a–h.

1 between 45 and 60
2 too heavy
3 not dangerous
4 over 80
5 spends money on others
6 has little or no hair
7 makes people laugh
8 healthy and gets regular exercise

a funny
b elderly
c safe
d in shape
e overweight
f middle-aged
g bald
h generous

3 Put the words in the correct columns.

overweight nursery curly college
straight kindergarten lazy unfriendly
school long ugly brown

Places of learning	Types of hair	Other adjectives

4 Complete the conversation with the words in the box.

lazy funny blond tall cheerful
long young short

Jack How's your new colleague?
Victoria She's really ¹_____ . Always telling jokes!
Jack Do I know her? What does she look like?
Victoria She's ²_____ and slim. Only about 1 m. 55.
Jack With ³_____ hair?
Victoria Not at all. She has short hair.
Jack Brown?
Victoria No. ⁴_____ , actually. What about your new boss?
Jack She's OK. She's ⁵_____ – only about thirty. She's pretty ⁶_____ – about 1 m. 70. She's ⁷_____ – you know, she smiles a lot. She works long hours. Not like the ⁸_____ manager we had before.

Lesson 9A List five school subjects.

Lesson 10A List five adjectives to describe places.

Lesson 9A Write two simple past questions about someone's school days.

Lesson 10A Write two sentences comparing two towns or cities.

Lesson 9B Write a sentence with *because*.

Lesson 10B List five adjectives to describe people's appearance.

Lesson 9C Write a question using *need to*.

Lesson 10C Write two sentences about you and your family with superlative adjectives.

Lesson 9D Think of five expressions for making suggestions.

Lesson 10C List five adjectives to describe personality.

Lesson 9D Think of three expressions for sounding sympathetic.

Lesson 10D Write a sentence with *when* to link two events in the past.

93

UNIT 11 On the move

LANGUAGE *have to/don't have to* ■ travel and transportation

11A Getting to work

1 A What forms of transportation can you see in pictures a–d? What other forms of transportation can you think of?

a

b

c

d

B How do you usually travel to these places? Tell a partner.

- your work or place of study
- your English class
- the supermarket

A *I always go to my English class by bus.*   B *Really? I drive.*

Go to Vocabulary practice: travel and transportation, page 155

2 A Read the introduction to the text. Complete the three definitions with the correct words.

1 _____ (verb): to travel to work
2 _____ (noun): the trip to work
3 _____ (noun): people who are traveling to work

B Read the rest of the text. Which forms of transportation does it mention?

THE WORLD'S coolest commutes

Do you have a long trip to work? Do you have to sit in traffic for hours or fight with thousands of other commuters for a place on the subway? It doesn't have to be stressful to commute. Here are three of the world's coolest commutes.

Chris Roberts is a doctor with Australia's Royal Flying Doctor Service. He spends about 90 minutes every day on a plane, and he often has to fly to some of the most remote places in Australia – places where there are no airports. "I love flying to work," he says, "but we have to look out for kangaroos when we land, especially at night."

Inger Bojesen is a journalist in Copenhagen, Denmark. Her trip to work is a 30-minute bike ride. In Copenhagen, 45% of people go to work by bike. There are bike lanes and special traffic lights for bicyclists, so they don't have to wait with all the cars and buses. And it's very safe. "I love my commute," says Inger. "It's really fast, and it's free!"

John Douglas is an engineer at a power plant on beautiful Lake Manapouri in New Zealand. There are no roads to the power plant, so John has to drive to the ferry, and then he and his coworkers have to travel across the lake by boat. It's called the "Z" boat because "zzzz" is the sound of workers sleeping during the trip! "It's a great way to start the day," says John.

3 Read the text again. Who do you think says the following about his/her commute: Chris, Inger, or John?

1 It's a really quiet commute, and the scenery is beautiful. _____
2 Sometimes I see some interesting animals during my trip. _____
3 I love getting some exercise on my way to work. _____
4 I take two different forms of transportation to get to work. _____
5 I can also go to work by car or bus if I want. _____
6 I travel at different times of the day. _____

94

have to/don't have to ■ travel and transportation   **LANGUAGE** **11A**

4 A Complete the sentences and question with words from the text.
1 We _____ look out for kangaroos when we land.
2 Bicyclists _____ wait with all the cars.
3 John _____ drive to the ferry.
4 _____ you _____ sit in traffic for hours?

B Choose the correct option. Then look at the examples in the Grammar box and check.
After *have to* or *has to*, we use the _____ base / -ing form of the verb.

> **Grammar** *have to/don't have to*
>
> We use *have to/has to* to say that something is necessary:
> We **have to go** there by plane.
> She **has to drive** to work.
> **Do** you **have to take** the train to work?
>
> We use *don't have to/doesn't have to* to say that something isn't necessary:
> You **don't have to go** to work by car.
> It **doesn't have to be** stressful to commute.

Go to Grammar practice: *have to/don't have to*, page 132

5 A ▶ 11.3 **Pronunciation:** *have to/has to* Listen and repeat.
1 I don't have to go by boat.
2 Do you have to work today?
3 He has to go by bike.
4 She has to get up early.

B ▶ 11.4 Say the sentences. Listen, check, and repeat.
1 You have to go to work by subway.
2 We don't have to work today.
3 She has to wear a uniform.
4 He doesn't have to go to school on Sundays.
5 Do you have to go home by bus?
6 Does she have to drive to work?

6 A Look at the signs and complete the sentences. Use the verbs in the box with *have to/don't have to*.

pay   turn off   leave

1 You _____ your phone.
2 You _____ to go in.
3 You _____ your dog outside.

B In pairs, explain what the signs mean. Use *have to* and *don't have to*.

a
b
c

Go to Communication practice: Student A page 165, Student B page 174

7 A Ask and answer questions about your partner's commute to work or place of study.
How do you get to work? I have to drive because there are no buses.

B Work with a different partner. Tell him/her about your first partner's trip.
Ana works at the airport. She goes there by subway. It's usually very busy, and she has to stand.

Personal Best Write a paragraph about your favorite form of transportation and why you like it.

11 SKILLS READING reading for detail ■ adverbs of probability

11B Looking for Elizabeth Gallagher

1 **A** Imagine you can go on a trip to anywhere in the world for three weeks. Write down the countries you'd like to visit.

B In pairs, compare your lists. Say one thing you'd like to do in each country.

2 Read the text about Jordan Axani and Elizabeth Gallagher. What was unusual about their trip?

Skill | reading for detail

When you read a text, first look at the pictures and title, and then skim the text to understand the main ideas. After that, read the questions carefully. Underline any key words. Find the part of the text with the information you need, and read it slowly and carefully. The questions may repeat key words from the text, or they may express the ideas in a slightly different way.

3 Read the Skill box. Answer the questions.
1. When did Jordan and his girlfriend's relationship end?
2. What did Jordan do about their vacation when their relationship ended?
3. What happened when Jordan placed an ad on Reddit?
4. How was Jordan and Elizabeth's relationship at the end of the trip?
5. What did Jordan do after the trip?

4 Match the questions to the paragraphs. Then write the answers.
1. How old is Jordan? _2_
2. How long was the around-the-world trip? _____
3. How many people responded to Jordan's ad? _____
4. Where did Jordan and Elizabeth spend New Year's Day? _____
5. Which city was Jordan and Elizabeth's favorite? _____

5 Read the Text builder. Complete the chart with the adverbs in the box.

Text builder | adverbs of probability

We use adverbs of probability to say how certain we feel about something.
Maybe and *perhaps* usually come at the beginning of a sentence:
Maybe one day there will be a movie about their adventures.

Other adverbs of probability usually come before the main verb, but after the verb *be*:
*Things **definitely** felt a little strange at first.*   *Prague was **possibly** their favorite place.*

definitely   maybe   perhaps   possibly   probably   certainly

It's certain	It's almost certain	It's not certain

6 **A** Look at the list of activities below. Check (✓) the ones you'd definitely like to do, put a question mark (?) next to the ones you'd possibly like to do, and a cross (X) next to the ones you definitely wouldn't like to do.

ride an elephant ☐   fly in a helicopter ☐   learn an instrument ☐
climb a volcano ☐   appear on TV ☐   run a marathon ☐
write a book ☐   learn a new skill ☐   do a parachute jump ☐

B Compare your ideas in pairs.

A *I'd definitely like to ride an elephant.*   B *Really? I definitely wouldn't want to do that! I'd like to climb a volcano.*

reading for detail ■ adverbs of probability **READING** SKILLS **11B**

LOOKING FOR
Elizabeth Gallagher

1 It's like a story in a movie: a couple plans a romantic trip around the world, but then they break up. The boyfriend doesn't want to go on the trip by himself, but he can't change the names on the tickets. He has to go alone … or he has to find another woman with the same name as his ex-girlfriend. So he starts looking for one …

2 That's exactly what happened to 28-year-old Jordan Axani from Canada. He reserved a three-week-long vacation with his girlfriend, but their relationship ended a month before the vacation started. Jordan didn't want to cancel his vacation but he didn't want to go alone. The airline told Jordan that it was impossible to change the names on the tickets, so he decided to find a woman with a Canadian passport and with the same name as his ex-girlfriend: Elizabeth Gallagher.

3 Jordan placed an ad on the website Reddit, and about 1,200 women contacted him. Of those 1,200 women, eighteen had the name Elizabeth Gallagher and a Canadian passport. Jordan chose a 23-year-old student from Nova Scotia to come with him on the trip.

4 Jordan and Elizabeth had an amazing trip; they saw some beautiful places and met some great people. They went to New York, Paris, Venice, and Bangkok. They spent the New Year in Hong Kong. Prague was possibly their favorite place. Did they become friends? Yes, they did. Elizabeth thought that things definitely felt a little strange at first, but, after a while, they were like brother and sister. Elizabeth had a boyfriend back in Canada, so she and Jordan probably got along better because of this.

5 So, what's next for Jordan and Elizabeth? Elizabeth went back to her life in Nova Scotia. But Jordan is writing a book and – who knows – maybe one day, there really will be a Hollywood movie about their adventures together.

Personal Best — Imagine you are Jordan or Elizabeth. Write an e-mail to a friend at home telling him/her about your trip.

11 LANGUAGE *be going to* and future time expressions ■ vacation activities

11C Road trip

1 A Complete the questions about vacations with the verbs in the box.

visit   go (x3)   relax   stay

1 Do you prefer to _____ to the beach or to the mountains?
2 Do you prefer to _____ at a hotel or at a campsite?
3 Do you prefer to _____ sightseeing or _____ by the pool?
4 Do you prefer to _____ a castle or _____ shopping for gifts?

B Ask and answer the questions in pairs.

Go to Vocabulary practice: vacation activities, page 156

2 Read the text. What is the connection between the two pictures?

RADIO 7
The best road trip

In the early 1940s, Sullivan Richardson, a journalist from Detroit, got into his white Chrysler with two friends and drove 14,000 miles from North America to the very tip of South America.

It's one of the greatest car adventures of all time. There were no roads for a lot of their trip. The three men drove over mountains and through deserts and jungles. At night, they camped next to the car. People said the trip was impossible, but after nine months and one day, they finally reached their destination in Chile. It was the trip of a lifetime! Now, more than 75 years later, friends Jack Reid and Ben Davis are going to take a similar trip along the longest road in the world – the Pan-American Highway, but in a comfortable camper!

3 ▶ 11.6 Listen to an interview with Jack and Ben. Complete the chart with information about the trip.

	Sullivan Richardson's trip	Jack and Ben's trip
Starting point	Detroit	1
Length of trip	nine months	2
Where / stay?	camped next to the car	3
Sightseeing?	no	4

4 A ▶ 11.6 Listen again and complete the sentences.
1 We're going to _____ from Arizona.
2 We're not going to _____ all the way to Chile.
3 Where are you going to _____?
4 Are you going to _____ the same places as Sullivan?
5 We're going to _____ a volcano in Guatemala.
6 We're going to _____ hiking in Costa Rica.

B Choose the correct options to complete the rules. Then read the Grammar box and check.
1 We use *be going to* to talk about the *present / future*.
2 After *be going to*, we use the *-ing / base* form of the verb.

be going to and future time expressions ■ vacation activities LANGUAGE **11C**

Grammar: *be going to* and future time expressions

We use *be going to* + the base form of the verb to talk about future plans:
I'm going to visit the beaches in Brazil.
We're going to drive 14,000 miles.
She's not / She isn't going to go by bus.
We're not / We aren't going to travel all the way to Chile.
Where are you going to stay?
Is your friend going to come with you?

Look! We use future time expressions with *be going to*.
She's going to get a new job **next year**.

Go to Grammar practice: *be going to* and future time expressions, page 133

5 A ▶11.8 **Pronunciation: sentence stress** Listen to the sentences. Listen again and repeat.
1 She's going to travel by train.
2 We're not going to go to the beach.
3 Are you going to stay with friends?

B ▶11.9 Say the sentences. Listen, check, and repeat.
1 I'm going to visit the castle.
2 You're not going to come with me.
3 We're going to travel by boat.
4 He's not going to relax by the pool.
5 Are you going to visit South America?
6 Is she going to stay at a hotel?

6 A Complete the conversation with the verbs in the box and the words in parentheses. Use *be going to*.

stay   visit   do   go (×2)   take   come   watch

Nuria Where ¹_____ (you and Tim) on vacation this year?
Mona Cape Town in South Africa.
Nuria Really? I went last year – it's amazing! What ²_____ (you) there?
Mona ³_____ (we) Robben Island, and ⁴_____ (we) hiking up Table Mountain. ⁵_____ (I) a rugby game, but ⁶_____ (Tim) with me – he's not interested in sports. I think ⁷_____ (he) some photos of the city.
Nuria It sounds great. Where ⁸_____ (you)?
Mona We're not sure yet. Do you know any good hotels?

B Act out the conversation in pairs.

Communication practice: Student A page 166, Student B page 175

7 A In pairs, plan your own "vacation of a lifetime." Make notes about your plans.

Which country? One place or different places? (forest, city, coast, etc.)	
Travel to your destination? (plane, ferry, car, etc.)	
Length of stay? (one week, two weeks, one month, etc.)	
Accommodations? (hotel, apartment, campsite, etc.)	
Places to visit? (museums, castles, stores, etc.)	
Activities? (sports, hiking, surfing, etc.)	

B Work with a different partner. Talk about your vacation plans. Ask him/her for more information.

A *We're going to go to China on vacation. We're going to stay there for two weeks, and we're going to visit a lot of different places.*
B *That sounds interesting. Which places are you going to visit?*

Personal Best You are going to go on a road trip. Write an e-mail to a friend about your plans for the trip.

11 SKILLS SPEAKING — arriving at a hotel ■ checking information

11D At a hotel

1 A Look at the reasons why people stay at hotels. Can you think of more?
- You're on vacation.
- You have a very early flight at an airport.
- You're on a business trip.

B In pairs, discuss the questions.
1. What do you enjoy about staying at hotels?
2. Is there anything that you don't like about hotels? What?
3. When did you last stay at a hotel? Describe your experience.

2 ▶ 11.10 Watch or listen to the first part of *Learning Curve*. Check (✓) the type of room that Ethan and Penny have.

	Standard room	Deluxe room
Ethan		
Penny		

3 ▶ 11.10 Watch or listen again. Are the sentences true (T) or false (F)?

1. Ethan's going to reserve a hotel room in New York. ____
2. He has a meeting there. ____
3. He reserves a room for three nights. ____
4. Breakfast is included in the price. ____
5. There's a discount for all the rooms. ____
6. Penny spells her first name for the receptionist. ____
7. Her room's on the seventh floor. ____

Conversation builder — arriving at a hotel

Hotel receptionist:
Welcome to the ... Hotel.
(Are you) Checking in?
Could you spell your last name, please?
Could/Can I have your identification/ID/credit card, please?
Can you sign this form, please?
Here's your room key/passport/credit card.

Hotel guest:
I reserved a room under/in the name of ...
I have a reservation under/in the name of ...
Which floor did you say?
What's the WiFi password?

4 A Read the Conversation builder. Order the sentences from 1–9 to make a conversation.

a ☐ Here you are. Here's my passport.
b ☐ Sure.
c ☐ OK. Here's your room key. Room number 1203, on the twelfth floor.
d ☐ Thank you. Could I have your ID, please?
e ☐ Thanks. Which floor did you say? The tenth?
f ☐ Great. Can I have your credit card, please?
g ☐ Yes. I reserved a room under the name of Lucía Espinosa
h ☐ No, the twelfth floor.
i ☐ Welcome to Park Road Hotel. Checking in?

B In pairs, act out the conversation. If you want, use your own names and change the other details.

arriving at a hotel ■ checking information **SPEAKING** **SKILLS** **11D**

5 ▶ 11.11 Watch or listen to the second part of the show. Who enjoyed their stay at the hotel? Who didn't enjoy it?

6 ▶ 11.11 Watch or listen again. Choose the correct options to complete the sentences.
1 Penny says she'd like to *check in / check out / change rooms*.
2 Penny's stay was *horrible / comfortable / lovely*.
3 Ethan paid *more than / less than / the same as* Penny.
4 The WiFi in Ethan's room was *awful / pretty good / very good*.

7 A Read the Skill box. Complete mini-conversations 1–4 with a phrase to check the information.

> **Skill** checking information
>
> If you aren't sure if information is correct, you can check it with the person who said it.
> **Formal:**
> *You're going on May 11. Is that correct?   He's over eighteen. Is that correct?*
> **Neutral:**
> *Did you say one room for one night?   Did you say the fourth floor?*
> **Informal:**
> *That's with the discount, right?   Breakfast is at seven, right?*

1 A I'd like to reserve a double room for two nights.
   B You want a double room. _____?
2 A I'd like a standard room for three nights. Arriving on April 19th.
   B _____ two nights from April 19th?
3 A The price for a deluxe room is $100 a night.
   B The price includes breakfast, _____?
4 A There's a 20 percent discount for advance reservations.
   B _____ a 20 percent discount?

B ▶ 11.12 Listen and check. Pay attention to the intonation. Then act out the conversations in pairs.

Go to Communication practice: Student A page 166, Student B page 175

8 A **PREPARE** In pairs, look at the diagram and discuss what you could say at each stage. You can make notes.

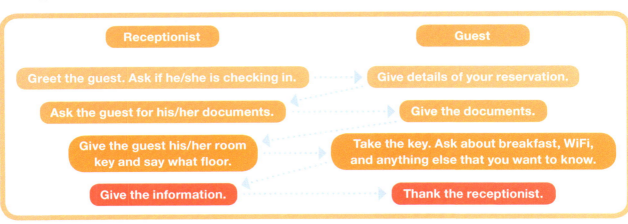

B **PRACTICE** Repeat the conversation until you can say it without looking at the diagram or your notes. Check any information that you're not sure about.

C **PERSONAL BEST** Work with another pair. Listen to their conversation. Did they check any information? What was good about their conversation?

Personal Best   Ethan is checking into a hotel in your town/city. Write the conversation.

101

UNIT 12

Enjoy yourself!

LANGUAGE present perfect with *ever* and *never* ■ entertainment

12A Going out

1 A Complete the chart with the words about entertainment.

fan   game   play   opera house   actor   club

People	Places	Events

B In pairs, add more words about entertainment that you know to the chart.

Go to Vocabulary practice: entertainment, page 157

2 A Read the interview. Who is the person in the picture? What is he going to try for the first time?

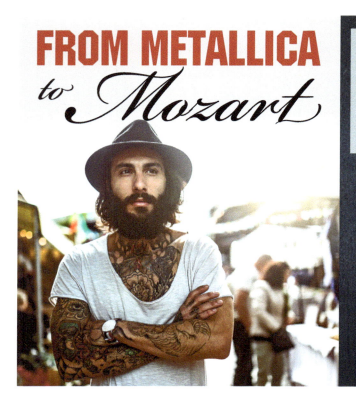

FROM METALLICA to Mozart

What happens when a heavy metal fan goes to an opera for the first time?
Have you ever been to a baseball game? Have you ever acted in a play? Is there a new experience that you'd like to try? Each week, we ask a guest to try something new for the first time. Our guest this week is Steve Bryant, a journalist with the heavy metal magazine, *Metal World*. Steve has never been to an opera.

So you've never been to an opera, Steve – is that right?
That's right. I've been to music festivals and rock concerts, but not to an opera. I've walked past the opera house, but I've never been inside.

We know you love heavy metal. What other music do you listen to?
I like a lot of different styles of music, from rock to blues and soul, and singer-songwriters like Neil Young and Bruce Springsteen.

What are your thoughts about opera music?
I've never really listened to it, and I don't know much about it. So this is going to be an interesting experience. I don't know if I'm going to like it!

B Read the interview again. Are the sentences true (T) or false (F)?

1 Steve has never been to a music festival. ____
2 Steve has never been inside an opera house. ____
3 He's only interested in heavy metal music. ____
4 He knows a lot about opera. ____

3 A Complete the sentences from the interview.

1 _____ you _____ to a baseball game?
2 Steve _____ never _____ to an opera.
3 I _____ past the opera house.
4 I _____ never _____ inside.

B Complete the rules. Then read the Grammar box.

1 We form the present perfect tense with the verb _____ + past participle.
2 We often use the adverb _____ in questions to ask about someone's experiences.
3 We often use the adverb _____ in negative sentences about experiences.

102

present perfect with *ever* and *never* ■ entertainment   LANGUAGE **12A**

📖 Grammar — present perfect with *ever* and *never*

We use the present perfect to talk about experiences in our lives.
Affirmative: *I've been* to music festivals and rock concerts.
Negative: *He hasn't listened* to an opera — *He's never listened* to an opera.
Questions: *Have* they *(ever) acted* in a play?   Yes, they *have*. / No, they *haven't*.

Look! Regular past participles are the same as simple past forms. They end in -*ed*: act*ed*, walk*ed*, listen*ed*.
The past participle of *go* is *gone*, but we often use *been* for experiences:
I went to London again last year. I've already been three times.

Go to Grammar practice: present perfect with *ever* and *never*, page 134

4 A ▶12.3 **Pronunciation:** sentence stress Listen and repeat.
1 I've been to an opera.
2 I haven't been to a tennis game.
3 I've never sung in a band.
4 Have you ever bought a lottery ticket?

B ▶12.4 Say the sentences. Listen, check, and repeat.
1 Have you ever been to New York?
2 I've acted in a play.
3 I've never had a pet.
4 I haven't flown business class.

5 ▶12.5 Listen to part 2 of the interview with Steve. Complete the sentences.
1 I _____ about going to an opera.
2 I _____ a lot of bands.
3 Now I can say that _____ to an opera!
4 Most of my colleagues _____ an opera.

6 A Complete the sentences with the past participles of the verbs in the box.

see   cook   work   fly   fail   go   cry   arrive

1 I've _____ during a movie.
2 I've never _____ a Shakespeare play.
3 I've _____ to a ballet.
4 I've never _____ an exam.
5 I've _____ Chinese food.
6 I've never _____ late for my English class.
7 I've _____ as a waiter in a café.
8 I've never _____ in a helicopter.

B In pairs, say which sentences are true for you.
A *I've cooked Chinese food.*   **B** *That's not true for me! I've never cooked it.*

Go to Communication practice: Student A page 166, Student B page 175

7 A In pairs, ask and answer the questions in the questionnaire.
A *Have you ever been to a soccer game?*   **B** *Yes, I have. How about you?*

Are you adventurous?

Do you like to try new things? How adventurous are you?
Try our questionnaire to find out.

HAVE YOU EVER ...
1 (go) to a soccer game?
2 (see) your favorite band in concert?
3 (be) in a carnival?
4 (play) in a band or orchestra?
5 (visit) an art gallery?
6 (go) to an opera?
7 (dance) salsa?
8 (climb) a mountain?

YOUR SCORE
7–8 You're very adventurous. Is there anything you haven't done?!
4–6 You're pretty adventurous, but there's a lot more that you can try in life.
1–3 You haven't done many things, but don't worry! Why not try something new this weekend?

B Find your partner's score and tell the class about him/her.
Sofia is pretty adventurous. She's been in a carnival, but she's never climbed a mountain.

Personal Best Write about five things that you have done this year.

12 SKILLS   LISTENING   listening for detailed information (2) ■ linking ■ opinion adjectives

12B The book was better!

1 Complete the sentences with the words in the box.

> terrible   sad   amazing   fun   scary   strange

1 This is _____!
2 This movie is really _____!
3 What a _____ picture!

4 Our team is _____ today.
5 This view is _____!
6 This book is so _____.

2 Think of an example for each of the adjectives in exercise 1. Tell your partner.

Walking in the forest at night is scary.

Go to Vocabulary practice: opinion adjectives, page 157

3 ▶ 12.7   Watch or listen to the first part of *Learning Curve*. Which sentence isn't true?

1 Kate knows more about *Frankenstein* than Simon.
2 There are lots of different *Frankenstein* movies.
3 *The Lord of the Rings* movies were created before the books.

Skill listening for detailed information (2)

It is often necessary to understand what someone says in detail.
- Listen carefully to all the speakers. Sometimes one person corrects another person's information.
- Listen for people's names. Often you hear important information about the person immediately after you hear the name.
- Listen for key nouns and adjectives.

4 A ▶ 12.7   Read the Skill box. Then read the sentences below and watch or listen again. Are the sentences true (T) or false (F)?

1 Kate says Dr. Frankenstein is a monster. ____
2 The most famous Frankenstein's monster is from the 1931 movie. ____
3 In the book, Frankenstein's monster never speaks. ____
4 Boris Karloff's special boots made the monster very tall. ____
5 There are three *The Lord of the Rings* books. ____
6 They made the first movie in 274 days. ____
7 Some characters are funnier in the movie than in the books. ____
8 The location of the films was Australia. ____

B In pairs, discuss *Frankenstein* and *The Lord of the Rings*. Have you seen or read them? If not, would you like to see or read them? What do you think of them?

listening for detailed information (2) ■ linking ■ opinion adjectives **LISTENING** **SKILLS** **12B**

5 ▶12.8 Watch or listen to the second part of the show. Choose the correct options to complete the sentences.

1 Andy thinks _____ is amazing.
   a *The Lord of the Rings*   b the original *Mad Max* movie   c the third *Mad Max* movie
2 Millie has seen all the *Harry Potter* movies _____ .
   a 10 times   b 15 times   c 20 times
3 Holly explains that Jane Austen didn't write _____ , but it has the same story as one of her books.
   a *Emma*   b *Clueless*   c *Pride & Prejudice*
4 Yiannis thinks that _____ were the best ones.
   a the first *James Bond* movies   b the first *James Bond* books   c the later *James Bond* movies

6 ▶12.8 Watch or listen again. Correct the mistakes in the sentences.
1 The original *Mad Max* movie is American.   _____
2 Andy says that *Mad Max: Fury Road* is a happy movie.   _____
3 In *Harry Potter*, they play Quidditch in the dining hall. _____
4 Charlie, Percy, and Bill are Ron Weasley's younger brothers. _____
5 The book *Emma* is about people in a high school.   _____
6 *Bridget Jones's Diary* was a movie before it was a book. _____
7 The first *James Bond* movies were very different from the books. _____
8 Ian Fleming was a spy in the *James Bond* books.   _____

7 A Make notes in the chart about some books you know that are also movies.

Book	Opinion of book	Movie	Opinion of movie

B In pairs, discuss the books and movies.
I love the book The Great Gatsby. It's beautiful and sad. But I think the 2013 movie is terrible.

Listening builder linking consonants and vowels

When a word ends in a consonant sound and the next word starts with a vowel sound, we usually link them together:
The Lord‿of the Rings was‿a very popular series‿of books.
I can talk‿about James Bond‿all day!

8 ▶12.9 Read the Listening builder. Look at the sentences from the program and mark the links between words. Then listen and check.
1 Let's talk about the movie of another book.
2 I thought it was exciting!
3 She's a big fan of Jane Austen's books.
4 I'm sure a lot of people agree with us!
5 I've read all the books and seen all the movies.

9 A Prepare a one-minute talk about a movie. Use these questions to help you.
• What is the movie about?   • Was the location important?   • Did the idea for the movie
• Who were the actors?   • What's your opinion of it?   come from a book?

B In pairs, give your talks. Ask your partner questions about his/her movie.

Personal Best Choose two films and write a paragraph comparing them. Which movie is better/sadder/more exciting/funnier? 105

12 LANGUAGE present perfect and simple past

12C A famous voice

1 A Look at the picture and answer the questions.
1 Who is the character on the right?
2 What cartoon series is he from? Have you ever seen it?
3 Who do you think the woman on the left is?

B Read the text and check your answers.

NANCY CARTWRIGHT

As one of the most famous voices in the world, Nancy is the voice of Bart Simpson, from the American TV cartoon, *The Simpsons*. Naughty schoolboy Bart and his family are some of the world's most popular TV characters. Listen to today's program to find out more.

2 A ▶ 12.10 Listen to the radio program. When did Nancy start playing Bart?

B ▶ 12.10 Listen again and answer the questions.
1 Who did Nancy want to play at first?
2 What awards has Nancy won?
3 Has she ever acted in a movie?
4 What did Nancy say about her job on *The Simpsons*?

3 A Look at the extracts from the program. <u>Underline</u> the present perfect sentences, and (circle) the simple past sentences.

> **Rob** When did Nancy start playing Bart?
> **Chrissie** She started playing Bart in 1987.
>
> **Rob** Has Nancy ever won an award?
> **Chrissie** Yes, she's won a lot of awards. In 1992, she won an Emmy.

B Answer the questions. Then read the Grammar box.
1 Which two time words does Rob use in the box above?
2 Which tense does he use with these time words?

📖 Grammar present perfect and simple past

Present perfect (talking about experiences in our lives, when we don't say when something happened):
She**'s acted** in movies.   I**'ve been** to New York.   **Have** you ever **won** an award?

Simple past (asking for and giving more detail about past events):
She **was** in Godzilla **in 1998**.   I **went** to New York **last year**.   I **went** with my dad.
When **did** she **win** an award?   **Did** you **have** a good time there?

Go to Grammar practice: present perfect and simple past, page 135

106

present perfect and simple past LANGUAGE **12C**

4 Match the base forms, simple past forms, and past participles. Which past participles are the same as the simple past forms?

buy – bought – bought

Base form	Simple past	Past participle
buy drink drive eat	ate met saw drank	won eaten met read
fly meet read see	wrote flew spoke wore	worn written flown spoken
speak wear win write	drove won read bought	driven bought drunk seen

5 A ▶ 12.12 **Pronunciation:** vowels Listen and repeat the past participles in exercise 4.

B ▶ 12.13 Make pairs of past participles with the same vowel sound. Listen, check, and repeat.

w<u>o</u>n, dr<u>u</u>nk

6 A Write the conversations in full. Use the present perfect and simple past.

1
A you / ever / meet / a famous actor?
B yes
A who / you / meet?
B I / meet / Salma Hayek / last year.
A oh, really? where / you / meet / her?
B I / meet / her on a flight from Paris to London.

2
A you / ever / try / dangerous sport?
B yes
A what / you / try?
B I / try / rock climbing.
A you / enjoy / it?
B yes, it / be / great!

B In pairs, act out the conversations. Ask more questions to get more information.

Go to Communication practice: Student A page 166, Student B page 175

7 A Check (✓) the sentences that are true for you.
1 I've had a big party at my house. ☐
2 I've walked out of a movie theater before the end of a movie. ☐
3 I've bought clothes online. ☐
4 I've stayed awake all night. ☐
5 I've tried a dangerous sport. ☐
6 I've traveled first class. ☐
7 I've sung on stage. ☐
8 I've been on TV or in a newspaper. ☐

B Now work in groups. Ask *Have you ever* questions about the activities. Then ask simple past questions to find out more.

(What …?) (When …?) (Where …?) (Who …?) (How …?) (How much/many …?) (Did you …?)

A *Have you ever had a big party at your house?*
B *Yes, I have.*
A *How many people did you invite?*

Personal Best Think of an interesting experience you've had. Write a conversation like in exercise 6 to explain what happened.

107

12 SKILLS WRITING writing and replying to an invitation ■ articles

12D Would you like to come?

1 Match pictures a–d with the events in the box. What other types of parties can you think of?

a housewarming party   a dinner party   a wedding reception   an office party

2 Look at the party invitation below. Why are Amy and Will having a party?

Amy and Will
are having a
going-away party

We'd love you to join us as we say "Goodbye U.S." and "Hello Australia!"

When: Saturday July 2nd, from 12:30 to 4:30 p.m.
Where: 17 Park Avenue
Children are welcome. No presents please.
RSVP: amyj81@net.com or 917-555-2392.

3 Now read three replies. Who is going to go to the party? Who can't go?

Dear Amy and Will,
Thanks so much for the invitation. I'm really sorry, but we can't make it because we're on vacation then. Hope you have a great time, and good luck in Australia! Keep in touch. We'd love to come and visit you!
Best wishes,
Kate and Ian xx

Hi Amy, hi Will,
Thank you for the invitation. We'd love to come to the party, and both of the kids would love to come, too! We can't wait to see you.
Lots of love,
Ed and Fiona

Dear Amy and Will,
Thanks very much for the invitation. I can definitely make it. I'm probably going to be a bit late as I'm going to drive back from Boston that day. Can I bring anything? Food? Something to drink?
All the best,
Jim

12D WRITING SKILLS
writing and replying to an invitation ■ articles

Skill writing and replying to an invitation

When you write an invitation, say what sort of party it is, where it is, what time it starts, and the date. Give people your contact details:
We're having a (going-away) party.
Hope you can come. / Hope you can make it.
Please reply. / RSVP (from the French expression: *répondez s'il vous plaît*)

When you reply, thank the person who has invited you, and accept or decline the invitation. If you decline, explain why you can't come:
I'd love to come.
I'd love to come, but ... / I'm really sorry, but we can't come.

4 A Read the Skill box. Then read the invitation and replies again, and answer the questions.
1 Which of the phrases do Amy and Will use?
2 Find another phrase to invite someone to a party.
3 Find another phrase for accepting an invitation.
4 Find another phrase for declining an invitation.

B Rewrite the replies. Use phrases from the Skill box.

a
Hi Amy and Will,
I can't come. ☹ Exam that day.
George

b
Amy, Will,
Thanks. See you on the 2nd.
Jess and Matt

Text builder articles: *a/an*, *the*, or no article

We use *a/an* before singular nouns when we talk about a person or thing for the first time:
*Amy and Will are having **a** going-away party.*

We use *the* if we have already mentioned the person or thing:
*We'd love to come to **the** party.*

We use no article when we talk about things in general:
I love parties!

5 Read the Text builder and complete the sentences with *a/an*, *the*, or – (no article).

Lucy	I moved into ¹_____ new apartment last week, and I'm having ² _____ housewarming party next Friday. Would you like to come?
Joe	I'd love to! What time's ³_____ party?
Lucy	It's at eight o'clock. ⁴_____ apartment is 12A, Lancaster Street.
Joe	Great. Do you like ⁵_____ cake?
Lucy	Yes! Especially chocolate cake.
Joe	Great. I can make ⁶_____ orange and chocolate cake for the party.

6 A PREPARE Choose a type of party from exercise 1 or use your own ideas. Plan the details of your party.

B PRACTICE Write an invitation to your event. Then exchange it with a partner and write two replies: one accepting and one declining the invitation. Use information and phrases from the Skill box and exercise 3 on page 108.

C PERSONAL BEST Read your partner's replies to your invitation. Do they use phrases from the Skill box? Do they use articles correctly? Which reply is better and why?

Personal Best Plan the perfect party. Who would you invite and what would you do?

11 and 12 REVIEW and PRACTICE

Grammar

1 Cross out (**X**) the sentence that is NOT correct.

1. a I have to get up early every morning. ____
   b I have got up early yesterday. ____
   c I got up early yesterday. ____
2. a You have to drive on the left in the UK. ____
   b I drove on the left when I was in the UK. ____
   c You haven't to drive on the left in the UK. ____
3. a What do you going to do next weekend? ____
   b Are you going surfing next weekend? ____
   c What are you going to do next weekend? ____
4. a How's she going to get there? ____
   b Who's she going to go with? ____
   c How long she's going to stay? ____
5. a Have you ever drove a Rolls Royce? ____
   b I've never driven a Rolls Royce. ____
   c I drove a Rolls Royce ten years ago. ____
6. a When have you see her? ____
   b Have you seen a famous person? ____
   c When did you see her? ____
7. a I went to Poland last year. ____
   b I've been to Poland twice. ____
   c I never gone to Poland. ____
8. a She wrote some famous poems. ____
   b She has wrote some famous poems. ____
   c She has written some famous poems. ____

2 Rewrite the sentences with the words in parentheses.

1. It's necessary for me to get up early. (have to)
   _____
2. You can choose to come or not. (have to)
   _____
3. I don't plan to get a new job next year. (not / going to)
   _____
4. I'm not hungry, so I don't want dinner. (not / going to)
   _____
5. The train always stops at the next station. (going to)
   _____
6. I went to Paris in 2010 and 2012. (have / twice)
   _____
7. I always go on vacation in my own country. (never / abroad)
   _____
8. She buys lottery tickets and isn't successful. (have / never)
   _____

3 Choose the correct options to complete the text.

Part-time teacher, part-time magician

Alan Jordan has two jobs. From Monday to Friday, he teaches in an elementary school where he ¹*has to / have to* teach seven-year-olds how to read, write, and count. In the evenings and on the weekends, he becomes Ali Giordano and performs magic tricks for his audience. I asked him about the two jobs.

Q Which job do you prefer?

A I like both jobs. In both, I ²*have to / have* stand up in front of a large group of people and tell them stories. They ³*don't have to / have to* listen carefully to me, and I ⁴*have to / has to* be careful with my words.

Q ⁵*Have you ever used / Did you ever used* magic with your students?

A Of course. Last week, ⁶*I have taught / I taught* a complete math class using playing cards. They ⁷*learned / have learned* arithmetic and saw magic at the same time.

Q Have you used magic in other lessons?

A Yes. For example, two weeks ago ⁸*I taught / I've taught* my class some vocabulary. I put words on cards, and the children had to find the objects. Some of them ⁹*have appeared / appeared* by magic in surprising places!

Vocabulary

1 Circle the word that is different. Explain your answer.

1	match	opera	actor	concert
2	boat	bike	ballet	bus
3	boring	stupid	awful	amazing
4	pool	campsite	hotel	apartment
5	hiking	exciting	surfing	sightseeing
6	beach	mountains	museum	artist
7	strange	interesting	fantastic	great
8	train	taxi	ferry	car

110

REVIEW and PRACTICE 11 and 12

2 Match definitions 1–8 with words a–h.

1 really fantastic
2 tourists like doing this
3 a form of classical dancing
4 you can do this on the beach
5 you can stay here on vacation
6 really bad
7 this transports passengers by sea
8 the opposite of interesting

a ballet
b relax
c campsite
d sightseeing
e amazing
f boring
g terrible
h ferry

3 Put the words in the correct column.

opera subway great plane
bus play amazing ballet
game exciting truck cool

Positive adjectives	Forms of transportation	Types of entertainment

4 Choose the correct options to complete the sentences.

Jack How was your weekend?
Victoria It was ¹*great / boring / terrible*. We went to Miami, saw a movie, and then had a nice meal.
Jack What was the movie like?
Victoria It was ²*boring / all right / exciting* with a fabulous car chase! Unfortunately, the ending was ³*interesting / stupid / amazing*.
Jack Really? That's too bad. And how was the meal?
Victoria We went to a ⁴*boring / cool / scary* restaurant. It's very fashionable, so it was expensive, but the food was good.
Jack Sounds great.
Victoria It certainly wasn't ⁵*strange / boring / stupid*. It was very crowded with fabulous music. What about your weekend?
Jack It was ⁶*all right / amazing / sad*. Nothing special. We went to a concert on Saturday.
Victoria How was it?
Jack ⁷*Great / Terrible / Exciting*! I don't really like classical music, and it lasted over three hours. It wasn't even a good orchestra. Luckily, we went to this ⁸*strange / boring / amazing* club afterwards.

Personal Best

Lesson 11A List five forms of transportation.

Lesson 12A Think of four places you can go to for entertainment.

Lesson 11A Write a sentence with *I don't have to*.

Lesson 12A Write a question with *ever*.

Lesson 11B Write two sentences, one with *definitely* and one with *possibly*.

Lesson 12A Write a sentence with *never* in the present perfect.

Lesson 11C Name six vacation activities.

Lesson 12C Think of three irregular past participles and their simple past forms.

Lesson 11C Write a sentence about a place you plan to go to this year.

Lesson 12D Think of two expressions for inviting someone to something.

Lesson 11D Give three expressions for checking information.

Lesson 12D Think of two expressions for accepting an invitation.

GRAMMAR PRACTICE

7A Countable and uncountable nouns + some/any

Countable nouns are things that we can count.

I have a brother.
There are two glasses on the table.
There are fourteen students in the class.

Countable nouns have a singular and a plural form. We can use *a/an* with the singular form.

Do you want a banana?
I like bananas.
We need an egg for this recipe.
We need three eggs for this recipe.

Uncountable nouns are things that we can't count. They usually don't have a plural form, and we can't use *a/an* with them.

I don't like cheese.
Do you like lemonade?
There's a lot of sugar in this cake.
We're having pasta for dinner.

some/any

We use *some* in affirmative statements with uncountable nouns and plural countable nouns. We use it when we don't say exactly how much or how many.

There's some juice in the fridge.
There are some apples in the bowl.

We use *any* in negative statements and questions with uncountable nouns and plural countable nouns.

There isn't any milk.
We don't have any oranges.
Do you have any money?
Are there any strawberries?

▶ 7.4

	Countable nouns		Uncountable nouns
	Singular	Plural	
+	There's **a** banana.	There are **some** bananas.	There's **some** water.
−	There's **no** lemon.	There aren't **any** lemons.	There isn't **any** coffee.
?	Is there **an** onion?	Are there **any** onions?	Is there **any** tea?

Look! We usually use *some* in questions when we offer something to someone.
Do you want some soup?
Would you like some carrots?

1 Look at the picture. Write *a*, *an*, or *some*.

1 _____ meat
2 _____ chocolate
3 _____ melon
4 _____ apple
5 _____ bread
6 _____ orange
7 _____ potatoes
8 _____ tomatoes

2 Complete the conversation with *a*, *an*, *some*, or *any*.

A What's for lunch? Is there [1]_____ pasta?
B No, there isn't [2]_____ pasta. But there's [3]_____ rice in the cupboard.
A Good. And do we have [4]_____ meat or fish?
B Yes, we have [5]_____ chicken and [6]_____ fish. There's [7]_____ green pepper and [8]_____ onion, too, but there isn't [9]_____ salad.
A No problem. We can buy [10]_____ salad at the market.

3 Make sentences. Add *a*, *an*, *some,* or *any*.

1 there / not / cheese / on this pizza
_____
2 you / have / tomatoes / ?
_____
3 there / milk / in the fridge
_____
4 we / not have / yogurt
_____
5 there / mushrooms / in the shopping bag
_____
6 there / water?
_____

◀ Go back to page 59

GRAMMAR PRACTICE

7C Quantifiers: (how) much, (how) many, a lot of, a few, a little

We use *how much* and *how many* to ask about quantity. We use *how much* with uncountable nouns and *how many* with countable nouns.

How much fish do you eat every week?
How many students are there in your class?

We use *a lot of* or *lots of* with countable and uncountable nouns to talk about large quantities. We can use them in affirmative sentences, negative sentences, and questions.

I eat a lot of fruit.
I don't eat a lot of apples.
Do you eat a lot of potato chips?

We use *a lot of* and *many* to ask about quantities. We use *a lot of* with uncountable nouns and *many* with countable nouns.

Do you drink a lot of juice?
Are there many/a lot of students in your class?

We use *not much* and *not many* in negative sentences to talk about small quantities. We use *not much* with uncountable nouns and *not many* with countable nouns.

There isn't much sugar in this cake.
I don't eat many potato chips.

We use *a few* and *a little* in affirmative sentences and questions to talk about small quantities. We use *a little* with uncountable nouns and *a few* with countable nouns.

I'd like a little milk in my coffee.
Would you like a little sugar in your coffee?
I eat a few pieces of fruit every day.
Are there a few eggs in the fridge?

▶ 7.8	Countable nouns	Uncountable nouns
Large quantities	There are **a lot of/lots of** crackers. Are there **many** crackers? Are there **a lot of/lots of** crackers?	There's **a lot of/lots of** cheese. Is there **a lot of/lots of** cheese?
Small quantities	There are **a few** crackers. There aren't **many** crackers. There aren't **a lot of** crackers. Are there **a few** crackers?	There's **a little** cheese. There's not **much** cheese. There's not **a lot of** cheese. Is there **a little** cheese?

Look! With *a lot of / lots of*, we don't say *of* if we don't say the noun.
Do you have any milk? *Yes, we have a lot.* NOT ~~Yes, we have a lot of.~~

1 Complete the questions with *How much* or *How many*.
1 _____ cups of coffee do you drink every day?
2 _____ sugar do you put in your coffee?
3 _____ time do you spend online every day?
4 _____ e-mails do you send every day?
5 _____ rooms are there in your home?
6 _____ water do you drink every day?
7 _____ brothers and sisters do you have?
8 _____ jewelry do you wear?

2 Choose the correct words to complete the sentences.
1 There isn't *much / a lot* cheese in the fridge.
2 I drink *a lot / a little* of tea every day.
3 My friends don't send me *much / many* messages.
4 I don't take *much / a little* sugar in my tea.
5 It's good to eat *a lot / a little* fish every week.
6 I have *much / lots of* cousins.
7 Do your children eat *a few / a lot of* fruit?
8 I drink *a little / a few* glasses of milk every day.

3 Look at the picture and complete the sentences with quantifiers.

1 There are _____ cups.
2 There isn't _____ cake.
3 There are _____ bottles of water.
4 There's _____ pizza.
5 There aren't _____ potato chips.
6 There's _____ salad.

◀ Go back to page 63

125

GRAMMAR PRACTICE

8A Past of *be*, *there was/there were*, and simple past: irregular verbs

We use the past of *be* and the simple past to talk about completed actions and situations in the past.

The past forms of the verb *be* are *was* and *were*.

Life was difficult in the 1930s.
Our house wasn't very big.
We were very happy.
We weren't rich.

▶ 8.2	I / he / she / it	you / we / they
+	I **was** busy last week.	We **were** busy last week.
−	He **wasn't** busy yesterday.	They **weren't** busy yesterday.

there was/there were

We use *there was/there were* to say that something existed in the past.

There was a TV in our living room.
There were two rooms in our apartment.

▶ 8.3	Singular	Plural
+	**There was** a fridge in our kitchen.	**There were** a lot of books in my bedroom.
−	**There was no/There wasn't** any freezer.	**There weren't** any CDs.

Simple past: irregular verbs

The verb *be* is irregular in the past. A lot of common verbs have an irregular simple past form, too.

We made a cake yesterday.
I had an English class last week.

We make the negative simple past form of all verbs with *didn't* + the base form of the verb.

We didn't make bread yesterday.
I didn't have a French class last week.

▶ 8.5	I / you / he / she / it / we / they
+	I **bought** a lot of books in the 1990s.
−	I **didn't buy** expensive clothes.

For a full list of irregular verbs, see page 176.

1 Complete the sentences with *was*, *wasn't*, *were*, or *weren't*.

  1 I _____ born in the U.S. I'm Canadian.
  2 Chris _____ at my house yesterday. He was at home.
  3 It _____ Friday yesterday. Today is Saturday.
  4 We _____ at the movies last night. We left at 10.00 p.m.
  5 The stores _____ open, so we didn't buy anything.
  6 There _____ any tickets, so we didn't go to the concert.
  7 Lucia _____ born in Uruguay in 1978.
  8 The market _____ busy this morning. It was so crowded.

2 Write the sentences in the negative.

  1 I had breakfast this morning.
  _____
  2 We read the newspapers yesterday.
  _____
  3 My dad made dinner last night.
  _____
  4 We bought a color TV in the 1970s.
  _____
  5 I was at home on Saturday.
  _____
  6 My parents were on vacation last week.
  _____

3 Complete the text with the past of *be* or the simple past of the verbs in parentheses.

In the 19th century, life [1]_____ (be) difficult for a lot of people. Usually homes [2]_____ (be) pretty small. There usually [3]_____ (not be) a bathroom in the house. People [4]_____ (not have) modern inventions like TVs or radios. They [5]_____ (not buy) many things, and there [6]_____ (not be) any computers. But people [7]_____ (read) books and children [8]_____ (have) toys.

◀ Go back to page 67

GRAMMAR PRACTICE

8C Simple past: regular verbs and past time expressions

We use the simple past to talk about completed actions and situations in the past.

With regular verbs, we usually add *-ed* to the base form of the verb.

My brother worked as a waiter in London for two years.
In the past, children played with traditional toys.
My brother wanted a bike for his birthday.
I finished my exams last month.

Spelling rules for regular affirmative simple past *-ed* endings

We usually add *-ed* to the verb.
work ⇨ worked   watch ⇨ watched

When a verb ends in *e*, we add *-d*.
dance ⇨ danced   live ⇨ lived

When a verb ends in consonant + *y*, we change the *y* to *i* and then we add *-ed*.
study ⇨ studied   try ⇨ tried

When a verb ends in vowel + *y*, we add *-ed*.
play ⇨ played   enjoy ⇨ enjoyed

When a verb ends in consonant + vowel + consonant, we usually double the final consonant and add *-ed*.
stop ⇨ stopped   plan ⇨ planned

We make the negative form of regular verbs with *didn't* + base form.

▶ 8.12 I / you / he / she / it / we / they

I **enjoyed** the meal.
I **didn't enjoy** the movie last night.
We **watched** the movie together.
We **didn't watch** TV.

Past time expressions

We often use past time expressions with the simple past to say when an action or situation happened.

I played tennis last week.
I played tennis yesterday morning.
I moved to Spain seven years ago.
In the 1920s, clothes were very different from now.

last	evening/night/week/month/year/spring/summer/fall/winter
yesterday	morning/afternoon/evening
two days / three weeks / five years	ago
in	1990/the 1930s/the 18th century

Look! *We can say either "yesterday evening" or "last evening."*

---

1 Complete the sentences with the verbs in the box. Use affirmative simple past forms.

| enjoy live play work listen watch |
| study want |

1 In his last job, Tony _____ at a bank.
2 We _____ to the news on the radio.
3 She _____ in Berlin in a great apartment.
4 Lena _____ to go out, but her friends were busy.
5 They _____ tennis in the park yesterday.
6 My parents _____ a movie online last night.
7 I _____ reading my new book on the weekend.
8 I _____ Spanish in Mexico a few years ago.

2 Complete the sentences with *yesterday*, *last*, *ago*, or *in*.

1 Emma called me _____ morning.
2 Cameron stayed with us _____ night.
3 I read four books on vacation _____ summer.
4 We moved to Chicago eight years _____.
5 My dad opened a restaurant _____ the 1980s.
6 We watched a terrible movie on TV _____ afternoon.
7 _____ 1969, a person walked on the moon for the first time.
8 Carmen finished college four months _____.

3 Write sentences. Use the simple past and complete the time expressions.

1 I / visit / China / 2013
_____

2 my family / live / in Australia / 1970s
_____

3 Lucas / not finish / his homework / night
_____

4 Sam and Ellie / celebrate / Sam's birthday / at a restaurant / two days
_____

5 the 1990s / a lot of people / listen to / dance music
_____

6 my brother / not want / to go to the movies / night
_____

◀ Go back to page 71

127

GRAMMAR PRACTICE

9A Past: questions

For the past of *be*, we form questions with *was/were* + subject.

Were you a good student?
Was your school near your home?
Were the exams very difficult?
Was English your favorite subject?

For the simple past, we form questions with *did* + subject + base form of the verb.

Did you study Spanish in school?
Did your parents go to college?
Did you have toast for breakfast today?

▶ 9.4		I / he / she / it	you / we / they
Verb *be*	?	**Was** the class interesting?	**Were** Tom and Mía in class yesterday?
	Y/N	Yes, it **was**. / No, it **wasn't**.	Yes, they **were**. / No, they **weren't**.
Other verbs	?	**Did** you **have** an English class last week?	
	Y/N	Yes, I **did**. / No, I **didn't**.	

We can put question words at the start of the question to ask for more information.

What was your favorite subject?
Where did you study?
Who was your favorite teacher?
Why did you study history?
When did you finish college?
How was your vacation?
How many students were there in your class?
How much did your dictionary cost?
How long did you stay?
How far did you go?

1 Complete the past questions with the words in parentheses.

1 _____ (be/it) sunny yesterday?
2 _____ (you/play) golf with Laura?
3 _____ (they/enjoy) the game?
4 _____ (be/Paul) good at golf?
5 _____ (you/like) the golf course?
6 _____ (be/it) busy?
7 _____ (be/your shoes) comfortable?
8 _____ (Paul/stay) with you on the weekend?

2 Write short answers to the questions in exercise 1.

1 Yes, _____.
2 Yes, _____.
3 Yes, _____.
4 No, _____.
5 Yes, _____.
6 No, _____.
7 No, _____.
8 No, _____.

3 Put the words in the correct order to make questions.

1 you / a / did / vacation / good / have / ?
_____

2 go / did / where / you / ?
_____

3 on the tour / how many / were / people / ?
_____

4 the / hotels / nice / were / ?
_____

5 have / did / what time / you / dinner in the hotel / ?
_____

6 food / like / the / you / did / ?
_____

7 stay / did / long / how / you / ?
_____

◀ Go back to page 77

GRAMMAR PRACTICE

9C Verb patterns: verb + infinitive

When we use two verbs together, we need to use the right form for the second verb.

We use an infinitive after some verbs. These verbs often (but not always) refer to plans for the future.

 9.8

We **want**		**go** to the movies tonight.
I **hope**		**see** you tomorrow.
We'**re planning**	to	**move** next year.
She'**d like**		**visit** the U.S.
My parents **need**		**buy** a new car.
I **intend**		**join** a gym.

Other verbs that are followed by an infinitive are: *begin, choose, continue, agree, decide, learn, prefer, offer, start*.

> **Look!** The verbs *begin* and *start* can be followed by an infinitive or the *-ing* form. The meaning is the same.
> *I began learning English when I was five.* / *I began to learn English when I was five.*
> *The bus didn't come, so we started walking home.* / *The bus didn't come, so we started to walk home.*

The full form of *'d like* is *would like*. It means the same as *want*, but it is more polite.

I'd like to see your house.
Would you like to come on vacation with me?

We can also say *'d love/would love* + infinitive.

I'd love to go to Australia one day.
Would you like to go to the beach today? Yes, I'd love to!

> **Look!** We use both an infinitive and the *-ing* form after *like* and *love*. The meaning is different from *'d like* / *'d love*.
> *We like to travel/traveling. We'd like to go to Australia next year.*
> *I love to play/playing soccer. I'd love to play for Real Madrid one day.*

1 Complete the sentences with the infinitive of the verbs in the box.

| check | get | start | run | lose | make | pass | talk |

1 I'm learning _____ jewelry.
2 She's planning _____ classes this fall.
3 Did he agree _____ to you about it?
4 Emilio wants _____ weight.
5 I need _____ my e-mails.
6 Lisa is planning _____ in shape this summer.
7 They decided _____ a marathon.
8 I hope _____ my exams this term.

2 Choose one or both options to complete the sentences.

1 He really doesn't like *to cook / cooking*.
2 I'd like *to change / changing* my diet.
3 Do you like *to play / playing* sports?
4 She'd love *to spend / spending* more time with her grandchildren.
5 I like *to earn / earning* lots of money.
6 Would you like *to make / making* some new friends?
7 He'd love *to go / going* to college.

3 Look at Gemma's New Year resolutions. Then write sentences using the verbs in parentheses.

1 She is planning to _____
2 _____
3 _____
4 _____
5 _____
6 _____
7 _____
8 _____

◀ Go back to page 81

129

GRAMMAR PRACTICE

10A Comparative adjectives

We use a comparative adjective + *than* to compare two things or people.

The park is nicer than the bus station.
Los Angeles is bigger than San Francisco.
The lasagna here is better than the chicken.

▶ 10.2   comparative adj + *than*

Adam is	**older than**	me.
Julie is	**friendlier than**	Laura.
Skiing is	**more dangerous than**	walking.

Spelling rules for comparative adjectives

When an adjective is one syllable, we add *-er*.
fast ⇒ faster   old ⇒ older

When a one-syllable adjective ends in *-e*, we add *-r*.
nice ⇒ nicer   safe ⇒ safer

When a one-syllable adjective ends in a consonant + vowel + consonant, we double the final consonant and add *-er*.
hot ⇒ hotter   big ⇒ bigger

When an adjective ends in consonant + *y*, we usually change the *y* to *i* and then we add *-er*.
easy ⇒ easier   friendly ⇒ friendlier   happy ⇒ happier
BUT *shy ⇒ shyer   dry ⇒ dryer*

When an adjective is two or more syllables, we usually use *more* + adjective.
dangerous ⇒ more dangerous   crowded ⇒ more crowded
modern ⇒ more modern

Some comparatives are irregular.
good ⇒ better   bad ⇒ worse   far ⇒ further/farther

> **Look!** With some two-syllable adjectives, we usually use *-er*, not *more*.
> *quiet ⇒ quieter   narrow ⇒ narrower*
>
> We can also use *less* + adjective + *than* to compare things.
>
> *I'm less stressed on the weekend than during the week.* = *I'm more relaxed on the weekend than during the week.*

We can add **much** and **a lot** before comparatives to show there is a big difference.
We can add **a little** or **a bit** before comparatives to show the difference is small.

much, a lot, a little, a bit

big difference:

New York is	**much**	bigger than Boston.
Skiing is	**a lot**	more dangerous than walking.

small difference:

Today is	**a little**	hotter than yesterday.
The café is	**a bit**	more crowded than the restaurant.

---

1 Complete the sentences with the comparatives of the adjectives in parentheses.

1 Do you think a walk on the beach is _____ than going to a bowling alley? (romantic)
2 The second date is usually _____ than the first! (easy)
3 Playing video games is _____ than watching TV. (exciting)
4 The apartments here are _____ than those downtown. (large)
5 Sneakers are _____ than sandals for long walks up mountains. (good)
6 It's usually _____ here in the spring than in the summer. (wet)
7 The movies are _____ than the theater. (cheap)
8 Calling someone the wrong name on a date is _____ than being a few minutes late. (bad)

2 Look at the pictures. Choose the correct words and include comparative adjectives to complete the sentences.

1 My hair was *a lot / a bit* _____ when I was younger.

Joe 8kg   Chris 16kg

2 Joe's suitcase is *much / a little* _____ than Chris's.

Mexico City 8938 km   Seoul 8867 km

3 Mexico City is *much / a little* _____ from London than Seoul.

◀ Go back to page 85

GRAMMAR PRACTICE

10C Superlative adjectives

We use a superlative adjective to say that something is more than all the others in a group.

New York is the biggest city in the U.S.
The park is the nicest place in my town.
The lasagna is the best thing on the menu.

We use *the* with superlative adjectives.

New York is the biggest city in the U.S. NOT ~~New York is biggest city in the U.S.~~

▶ 10.11   *the* + superlative adj

Adam is	**the** oldest person	in our class.
Julie is	**the** friendliest person	that I know.
Skiing is	**the** most dangerous	sport.

Spelling rules for superlative adjectives

When an adjective is one syllable, we add *-est*.
fast ⇒ *fastest*   *old* ⇒ *oldest*

When a one-syllable adjective ends in *-e*, we add *-st*.
nice ⇒ *nicest*   *safe* ⇒ *safest*

When a one-syllable adjective ends in consonant + vowel + consonant, we double the final consonant and add *-est*.
hot ⇒ *hottest*   *big* ⇒ *biggest*

When an adjective ends in consonant + *y*, we usually change the *y* to *i* and then we add *-est*.
easy ⇒ *easiest*   *friendly* ⇒ *friendliest*   *happy* ⇒ *happiest*
BUT *shy* ⇒ *shyest*   *dry* ⇒ *dryest*

When an adjective is two or more syllables, we use *most* + adjective.
dangerous ⇒ *most dangerous*   *crowded* ⇒ *most crowded*
modern ⇒ *most modern*

For some two-syllable adjectives we don't use *most*.
clever ⇒ *cleverest*   *quiet* ⇒ *quietest*   *narrow* ⇒ *narrowest*

Some superlatives are irregular.
good ⇒ *best*   *bad* ⇒ *worst*   *far* ⇒ *furthest/farthest*

Look! If we use a possessive adjective directly before the superlative, we don't include *the*.
Emily is my best friend.
What's your most expensive possession?

---

1 Complete the sentences with the superlatives of the adjectives in parentheses.

1. She's _____ girl that I know. (pretty)
2. My friend Sam was _____ person in my class. (popular)
3. My son's _____ child in the world! (beautiful)
4. _____ month of the year here is February. (hot)
5. Singing in a band is _____ thing that I do. (exciting)
6. When was _____ day of your life? (happy)

2 Complete the sentences with the superlatives of the adjectives in the box.

| romantic   smart   nice   kind   expensive   noisy |

1. _____ piece of jewelry is this necklace. It cost more than 100 dollars.
2. You're _____ person that I know. You understand things very quickly.
3. My sister is _____ person in my family. She helps older people with their shopping.
4. _____ place at school was the cafeteria. Everybody talked there!
5. Mr. and Mrs. Brown are _____ neighbors. They're really lovely people and friendly, too.
6. Sam often gives his girlfriend Katia flowers. He's _____ of all my friends.

3 Look at the pictures and complete the sentences with comparative or superlative adjectives.

| big   small |

700 students   500 students   1000 students
Anna   **Jodie**   **Fumiko**

1. Anna's school is _____ than Jodie's.
2. Jodie's school is _____.
3. Fumiko's school is _____.

| good   bad |

Michael   **Jack**   **Matt**

4. Matt got _____ grades than Jack on his exams.
5. Michael got _____ grades.
6. Jack got _____ grades.

◀ Go back to page 89

131

GRAMMAR PRACTICE

11A have to/don't have to

We use *have to* + the base form of the verb to say that something is necessary.

We have to wear a uniform in school.
I have to go to work by bus.
My brother has to get up at 5:30 every morning.
Donna has to call her parents every night.

We use *don't have to* + base form to say that something isn't necessary.

I don't have to work on Mondays.
They don't have to study today. It's Sunday.
Carlotta doesn't have to buy a new computer. She got one for her birthday.
Simon doesn't have to cook dinner tonight. He's at a restaurant.

We use *have to/don't have to* for situations in the present and in the future.

I have to wear a uniform at work. (present situation)
I don't have to get up early tomorrow. (future situation)

▶ 11.2	I / you / we / they	he / she / it
+	I **have to work** tomorrow.	Jack **has to take** the train to work.
–	I **don't have to work** on Sunday.	He **doesn't have to start** work at 7:30.
?	Do you **have to take** the train today?	Does he **have to wear** a uniform?
Y/N	Yes, I **do**. / No, I **don't**.	Yes, he **does**. / No, he **doesn't**.

Look! We use *had to/didn't have to* to say that something wasn't necessary in the past.
I had to visit my aunt every weekend.
We didn't have to play sports after school.

---

1 Choose the correct words to complete the sentences.
 1 I *have to / don't have to* drive to work because there are no buses or trains near my house.
 2 We bought our train tickets online so we *have to / don't have to* buy them at the station.
 3 Visitors to our office *have to / don't have to* sign the visitors' book. They can't go into the building if they don't sign it.
 4 Elena is a waitress and she usually *has to / doesn't have to* work on the weekend because it's a busy time at the restaurant.
 5 You *have to / don't have to* wash those cups. Put them in the dishwasher!
 6 We *have to / don't have to* walk the dog twice a day because he needs the exercise.
 7 My brother *has to / doesn't have to* go far to work. His office is only about a kilometer from his home.
 8 My parents *have to / don't have to* teach me to drive, but they're giving me a lot of lessons at the moment!

2 Complete the sentences with the correct form of *have to* or *don't have to*.
 1 I'm sorry. I can't talk now. I _____ go!
 2 "_____ you _____ get up early to go to work?" "Yes. I get up at five."
 3 Matt _____ get in shape. He already swims, runs, and plays soccer every week.
 4 You _____ make dinner. I can do it.
 5 _____ children _____ go to school when they're five?
 6 My sister _____ teach in a school as part of her degree in education.
 7 We _____ stay at home. Do you want to go for a walk?
 8 What train _____ Paul _____ catch in the morning?

3 Look at the job information. Complete the sentences with *have to* or *don't have to* and the verbs from the box.

a uniform ✘	clothes from the store ✔
clothes at full price ✘	customers ✔
after 6 p.m. ✘	on the weekend ✔
a degree ✘	18+ ✔

buy   have   work (x2)   wear (x2)   be   serve

 1 You _____ a uniform.
 2 You _____ clothes from the store, but you _____ our clothes at full price. You get 50% off.
 3 You _____ customers.
 4 You _____ on the weekend, but you _____ after 6 p.m.
 5 You _____ over 18, but you _____ a degree.

◀ Go back to page 95

GRAMMAR PRACTICE

11C *be going to* and future time expressions

We use *be going to* + the base form to talk about future plans.

I'm going to visit friends in Mexico this year.
He's going to have pizza for dinner tonight.
We're not going to stay at a hotel.
What are you going to do this summer?

▶ 11.7	I	he / she / it	you / we / they
+	I'm going to relax by the pool.	She's going to stay at a campsite.	We're going to visit a museum.
–	I'm not going to study this weekend.	She's not/She isn't going to stay at an apartment.	My friends aren't going to visit me next year.
?	Am I going to meet your friends later?	Is she going to stay at a hostel?	Are they going to eat out tonight?
Y/N	Yes, I am. / No, I'm not.	Yes, she is. / No, she's not/she isn't.	Yes, they are. / No, they're not/ they aren't.

Look! When the main verb is *go*, we do not normally use *to go* after *going*.
Are you going surfing tomorrow?
Camille is going abroad next year.

But it is also correct to use *to go*.
Are you going to go surfing tomorrow?
Camille is going to go abroad next year.

Future time expressions

We often use the following future time expressions with *be going to*:

this	morning / afternoon / evening / week / weekend / month / year / spring / summer / fall / winter / January, etc.
tomorrow	morning / afternoon / evening / night
next	week / month / year / spring / summer / fall / winter / January, etc.
in	the morning / afternoon / evening / spring / summer / fall / winter / January, etc.

Look! We say *tonight*, NOT ~~this night~~.

Today is Monday, January 1st.

Monday	January 1st	this week	this morning	tonight
Tuesday	January 2nd		tomorrow morning	tomorrow night
Wednesday	January 3rd			
Thursday	January 4th			
Friday	January 5th			
Saturday	January 6th	this weekend		
Sunday	January 7th			
Monday	January 8th		next Monday	next Monday night

---

1 Write sentences. Use *be going to*.

  1 Mark / play / guitar / this evening
  _____
  2 my parents / go / vacation / tomorrow
  _____
  3 my sister / not run / a marathon / this summer
  _____
  4 I / cook / dinner / tonight
  _____
  5 you / go / swimming / this afternoon?
  _____
  6 we / not use / our car / this year
  _____

2 Jamie, Fran, Paola, and Alfredo are on vacation together. Complete the conversation with the correct form of *be going to* and a verb from the box.

read visit play relax not do take (x2) do go

Jamie What ¹_____ you and Alfredo _____ tomorrow?
Paola In the morning, we ²_____ sightseeing in the city. We ³_____ the castle and go shopping. What about you?
Jamie We ⁴_____ running, and then we ⁵_____ by the pool. In the afternoon, Fran ⁶_____ a surfing class, and I ⁷_____ my book on the beach.
Paola ⁸_____ Fran _____ a surfing class every day?
Jamie Yes, she is. She really wants to learn.
Paola Don't you want to?
Jamie No, I just want to relax. I ⁹_____ much this week. Just a bit of running and swimming.
Paola What about volleyball? Alfredo ¹⁰_____ volleyball this evening. Are you interested?
Jamie Yeah! Thanks!

3 Today is Monday, March 10th. Write the time expressions for the days and times.

  1 the morning of March 11th _____
  2 March 17–23rd _____
  3 March 10–16th _____
  4 the evening of March 10th _____
  5 April _____
  6 Saturday, March 15th and Sunday, March 16th _____

◀ Go back to page 99

133

GRAMMAR PRACTICE

12A Present perfect with *ever* and *never*

We use the present perfect to talk about experiences in our lives.

I've visited China.
He hasn't been to Australia.
Have you worked in a restaurant?

We often use *ever* in a question with the present perfect. It emphasizes that we are talking about "our whole lives up to now."

Have you ever listened to classical music?
Have your parents ever been to a festival?

We often use *never* to make a negative sentence with the present perfect. It emphasizes that we are talking about "our whole lives up to now."

I've never tried Russian food.
He's never been to Scotland.

We form the present perfect with the verb *have* and the past participle of the main verb.

▶ 12.2	I / you / we / they	he / she / it
+	I've **visited** a lot of castles.	He's **been** to Vietnam.
–	They **haven't studied** Italian.	She **hasn't played** badminton.
?	**Have** you **stayed** in this hotel?	**Has** he **worked** in London?
Y/N	Yes, I **have**. / No, I **haven't**.	Yes, he **has**. / No, he **hasn't**.

For regular verbs, the past participle form is the same as the past simple form. It ends in *-ed*. See page 127 for the spelling rules for simple past forms ending in *-ed*.

Look! In the present perfect, we use the past participle *-ed* form for negative sentences and questions, as well as affirmative sentences. This is different from the simple past, where we only use the simple past *-ed* form for affirmative sentences. Compare:
Did you visit the National Gallery yesterday?
Have you visited the National Gallery? NOT ~~Have you visit the National Gallery?~~
I didn't visit the National Gallery yesterday.
I haven't visited the National Gallery. NOT ~~I haven't visit the National Gallery.~~

Like the simple past, a lot of common verbs have an irregular past participle. For a full list of irregular verbs, see page 176.

Look! When we talk about experiences, we sometimes use *been to* instead of *gone to* to say that someone went somewhere and returned.
She's been to London three times. = (She went and returned.)

1 Choose the correct words to complete the sentences.
 1 Lev *has / have* worked as a professional dancer.
 2 I've *never / ever* been to an opera.
 3 I *has / have* acted in a few plays.
 4 *Have you ever / Have ever you* listened to jazz?
 5 Tom doesn't work here. He's *been / moved* to a different company.
 6 We've *ever / never* visited the museum in my town.

2 Complete the sentences with the past participles of the verbs in parentheses.
 1 I've never _____ a foreign language. (study)
 2 I've _____ in a restaurant, but I've never _____ in a store. (work)
 3 Have you ever _____ volleyball? (play)
 4 Has your mother-in-law ever _____ with you? (stay)
 5 I've never _____ to a classical concert. (be)
 6 We've never _____ a famous person. (see)
 7 We've never _____ together. (act)
 8 My sisters haven't _____ me in New York. (visit)
 9 I've _____ a lot of Indian food. (cook)

3 Write short conversations. Use the present perfect.

1
A you / ever / go / to Peru?

B no / I / never / go / to South America

2
A your mom / ever / study / English?

B yes / and / she / study / German, too

3
A Charlie and Kate / ever / play / rock music?

B no / but / they / play / classical music

◀ Go back to page 103

12C Present perfect and simple past

We use the present perfect to talk about an experience in our lives. We use the present perfect to introduce a topic and say that it happened.

I've met Jennifer Lawrence.
I've been to New York.
My sister has started a new job.

When we give details about the experience (for example, when something happened, what exactly happened, who you were with, or how you felt), we use the simple past.

I've met Jennifer Lawrence. I met her in a hotel in London.
I've been to New York. I went there in 2005.
My sister has seen a shark. She was really scared.

When we ask for more details about past events, we usually use the simple past, not the present perfect.

Where did you meet Jennifer Lawrence? NOT ~~Where have you met Jennifer Lawrence?~~
When did you go to New York? NOT ~~When have you been to New York?~~
How did your sister feel? NOT ~~How has your sister felt?~~

We often start a conversation with the present perfect. When we give details about the experience, or ask for them, we change to the simple past.

▶ 12.11

Situation	Form	Example
Question about an experience	Present perfect	**Have** you ever **been** to Spain?
Answer	Present perfect	Yes, I **have**.
Details	Simple past	I **went** there two years ago.
Question asking for details	Simple past	**Did** you **go** to Madrid?
Answer	Simple past	No, I **didn't**. But I **went** to Valencia and Málaga.

For a full list of irregular verbs, see page 176.

GRAMMAR PRACTICE

1 Choose the correct words to complete the conversation.
A ¹*Have you ever been / Did you ever go* to Peru?
B Yes, I have. ²*I've been / I went* with some friends from college last year.
A Where ³*have you been / did you go*?
B To Machu Picchu. ⁴*It's been / It was* fantastic.
A I'd love to go there! ⁵*I've been / I went* to Lima in 2010, but not Machu Picchu.
B Machu Picchu is amazing! ⁶*We've had / We had* a great time.
A What ⁷*have you done / did you do* there?
B ⁸*We've been / We went* on some incredible hikes.

2 Complete the conversation with the words in parentheses using the present perfect or the simple past.
A ¹_____ (you / ever / see) the movie *Selma*?
B Yes. I ²_____ (see) it in 2015.
A ³_____ (you / like) it?
B Yes, it ⁴_____ (be) great. David Oyelowo ⁵_____ (play) Martin Luther King Jr. very well.
A ⁶_____ (he / win) any awards?
B Yes, he ⁷_____ (win) some awards.
A ⁸_____ (he / be) in other movies?
B Yes. He ⁹_____ (be) in *Lincoln*. I ¹⁰_____ (love) that movie!

3 Write the conversation. Use the present perfect and the simple past.

A you / ever / do / karate?
_____
B yes / I / try / it / two years ago
_____
A what / you / think / of it?
_____
B I / really / like / it
_____
A where / you / learn?
_____
B I / take / classes at the sports center
_____

◀ Go back to page 107

VOCABULARY PRACTICE

7A Food and drink

1 🎧 7.1 Complete the food groups with the words in the box. Listen and check.

| cabbage | cereal | cookies | eggs | fish | grapes | juice | melon |
| mushrooms | onion | orange | peas | potato chips | rice | tea | yogurt |

fruit
1 pear   2 apple   3 banana   4 lemon   5 strawberry   6 _____   7 _____   8 _____

vegetables
9 pepper   10 carrot   11 beans   12 tomato   13 cucumber   14 potato   15 _____   16 _____   17 _____   18 _____

grains
19 pasta   20 bread   21 _____   22 _____

protein and dairy
23 meat   24 beef   25 cheese   26 ice cream   27 milk   28 _____   29 _____   30 _____

snacks and others
31 cake   32 salad   33 French fries   34 soup   35 _____   36 _____

drinks
37 coffee   38 cola   39 _____   40 _____

2 Read the definitions and write the words.

1 A small yellow fruit. _____
2 Food for breakfast. We usually eat it with milk. _____
3 A white vegetable. We often cook with it. _____
4 A cold brown drink. _____
5 Very small green vegetables. _____
6 The meat from a cow. _____
7 An orange vegetable. _____
8 A small green or purple fruit. _____
9 A large green vegetable. _____
10 A large green or yellow fruit. _____

147 ◀ Go back to page 58

VOCABULARY PRACTICE

7C Containers and portions

1 ▶ 7.6 Match the phrases in the box with pictures 1–15. Listen and check.

| a bar of | a bag of | a bottle of | a bowl of | a box of | a can of (x2) | a carton of |
| a cup of | a glass of | a jar of | a packet of | a piece of | a slice of | a spoonful of |

 1 _____ tea

 2 _____ bread

 3 _____ juice

 4 _____ tomatoes

 5 _____ cookies

 6 _____ cereal

 7 _____ cheese

 8 _____ pasta

 9 _____ olive oil

 10 _____ honey

 11 _____ carrots

 12 _____ chocolate

 13 _____ water

 14 _____ cola

 15 _____ sugar

2 Choose the food or drink that isn't possible.
1 a bowl of *soup / ice cream / cola*
2 a jar of *olives / jam / meat*
3 a bag of *cookies / apple juice / potato chips*
4 a slice of *yoghurt / cake / apple*
5 a can of *peas / tomatoes / sugar*
6 a carton of *cereal / juice / milk*
7 a piece of *cheese / meat / tea*
8 a cup of *coffee / potato / water*
9 a can of *honey / cola / lemonade*
10 a spoonful of *oil / honey / cheese*

3 Complete the sentences with the correct words.
1 I have two or three _____ of coffee every day.
2 How many _____ of bread do you want?
3 There are two _____ of lemonade in the fridge.
4 We need a big _____ of apple juice.
5 I have a _____ of cereal in the cabinet, but I don't want it.
6 We love olives, so we always have a few _____ in the cabinet.
7 It's very hot. I need a _____ of water.
8 If I want a snack, I buy a _____ of chocolate.
9 There's a _____ of strawberry jam, if you want some on your toast.
10 I sometimes buy a _____ of potato chips for my daughter.

◀ Go back to page 63

VOCABULARY PRACTICE

8A Inventions

1 ▶ 8.1 Match the words in the box with pictures 1–18. Listen and check.

| freezer | color TV | smartphone | fridge | digital camera | cassette player | dishwasher | (clothes) dryer | DVD player |
| black-and-white TV | laptop | GPS | toaster | video player | microwave | CD player | vacuum cleaner | washing machine |

1 _____ 2 _____ 3 _____ 4 _____
5 _____ 6 _____ 7 _____
8 _____ 9 _____ 10 _____ 11 _____
12 _____ 13 _____ 14 _____
15 _____ 16 _____ 17 _____ 18 _____

2 Match the words from exercise 1 with the descriptions below.

1 You use this to watch a show. _____, _____, _____
2 You keep food in this. _____, _____
3 You use this to cook food. _____, _____
4 You use this after you wash clothes. _____
5 You use this to listen to music. _____, _____, _____
6 You can use this to help you find a place. _____, _____
7 You can use this if you want to watch a movie. _____, _____, _____
8 You can use the Internet on this. _____, _____
9 You can take photos with this, but you can't use the Internet. _____
10 You can use this to wash plates and cups. _____

◀ Go back to page 66

VOCABULARY PRACTICE

8B Life stages

1 ▶ 8.7 Match the words and phrases in the box with pictures 1–12. Listen and check.

| be born   meet someone   get divorced   finish school   go to college   retire |
| have a baby/family   start school   get married   get a job   get a degree   die |

2 Complete the sentences with phrases in the correct form.

1. My dad _____ last year. But he's still really busy all the time!
2. My sister and my brother-in-law want to buy a big house with lots of bedrooms before they _____.
3. In the U.S., children _____ when they are five years old.
4. These days, a lot of people use the Internet to try to _____ special.
5. Dani doesn't want to _____ after he finishes school. He wants to start working, instead.
6. Jenny is in college. She wants to _____ in French and Russian.
7. My friends Emily and Martyn _____ last year on a beach in the Caribbean! It was beautiful!
8. Most women have babies in the hospital, but my dad _____ at home.

◀ Go back to page 68

8B Irregular verbs

1 ▶ 8.9 Match the irregular simple past forms in the box with the verbs. Listen and check.

| spoke   heard   said   began   had   ate   drank   left |
| thought   gave   drove   did   saw   got   came   took |
| went   met   wrote   knew |

1. begin _____
2. come _____
3. do _____
4. drink _____
5. drive _____
6. eat _____
7. go _____
8. give _____
9. hear _____
10. know _____
11. say _____
12. see _____
13. leave _____
14. speak _____
15. get _____
16. take _____
17. think _____
18. write _____
19. meet _____
20. have _____

2 Complete the text with the simple past forms of the verbs in the box.

| have   drive   leave   come   do   get (x2)   know   take   meet |

This is my family, and I'm Australian, but my dad is British. He ¹_____ the UK, and ²_____ here in 1985. He ³_____ a job in Sydney because he ⁴_____ some people there. He ⁵_____ my mom. They ⁶_____ married and ⁷_____ two children – my brother and me. They ⁸_____ a lot of things with us and ⁹_____ us to lots of beautiful places. We ¹⁰_____ from Sydney to Melbourne once, and another time from Sydney to Brisbane, in our old car!

◀ Go back to page 69

150

VOCABULARY PRACTICE

9A School subjects and education

1 ▶ 9.1 Match the school subjects in the box with pictures 1–15. Listen and check.

art biology chemistry geography history IT (information technology) literature math (mathematics) foreign languages music PE (physical education) physics science social studies technology

2 ▶ 9.2 Match the parts of the phrases. There are usually two or more possible matches. Listen and check.

1 pass
2 take
3 go to
4 do
5 get into
6 fail

a nursery school
b kindergarten
c elementary school
d middle school
e high school
f college
g an exam
h a test
i homework

3 Complete the definitions with words from exercises 1 and 2.

1 Very young children go to learn in these places. _____, _____
2 In this subject, you learn about the past. _____
3 In this subject, you read books and plays. _____
4 In this subject, you play different kinds of sports. _____
5 This verb means "get a bad result." _____
6 This is where you can study after you finish high school. _____
7 This verb means "get a good result." _____
8 In this subject, you learn about different animals and plants. _____
9 In this subject, you learn how to communicate with people in different countries. _____
10 Children go to learn in these places between the ages of 12 and 18. _____, _____

◀ Go back to page 76

VOCABULARY PRACTICE

9C Resolutions

1 ▶ 9.6 Write the phrases under the headings. Listen and check.
1 be (more) organized
2 buy (a car)
3 get (more) exercise
4 earn (more) money
5 get a (new) job
6 get in shape
7 have an interview
8 improve your diet
9 improve your relationship
10 join a gym
11 lose weight
12 make (new) friends
13 meet someone new
14 run a marathon
15 save (more) money

health
_____
_____
_____

money
_____
_____
_____

work and study
_____
_____
_____

relationships
_____
_____
_____

2 Choose the correct verbs to complete the sentences.
1 I want to *get* / *go* in shape this year.
2 My brother *improved* / *saved* a lot of money last year and bought a new house.
3 I want to *get* / *make* a new job this year because I don't like my job.
4 My boyfriend and I don't *make* / *get* much exercise. We're lazy!
5 If you want to *join* / *lose* weight, you need to get some exercise.
6 Kelly *is* / *does* very organized. She has a to-do list.
7 Do you know a good way to *see* / *make* new friends?
8 I don't *earn* / *do* much money. I want a new job!

3 Match the sentences.
1 I want to improve my relationship with my girlfriend.
2 I want to join a gym.
3 Last year, I decided to improve my diet.
4 I want to meet someone new this year.
5 I really don't like having interviews.

a I play soccer and I want to get in shape for that.
b I didn't have a boyfriend last year.
c I don't like answering questions about myself.
d I started eating a lot more fresh vegetables.
e I didn't spend much time with her last year.

◀ Go back to page 80

10A Adjectives to describe places

1 ▶ 10.1 Match the adjectives with the correct pictures. Listen and check.

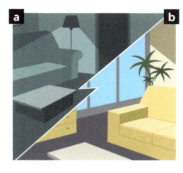 

1 dark _____   3 empty _____
2 light _____   4 crowded _____

5 friendly _____   7 lovely _____
6 unfriendly _____ 8 horrible _____

 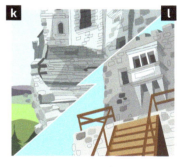

9 beautiful _____   11 safe _____
10 ugly _____   12 dangerous _____

2 Complete the sentences with adjectives from exercise 1.
1 Why is this restaurant _____? Perhaps the food's not good.
2 We love living in this area because it's _____ for the children to play outside.
3 People are _____ in small towns. They always say "hello."
4 I usually walk to work. There's a bus, but it's always _____ and you can't get a seat.
5 The outside of our apartment building is a bit _____, but it's not a problem. You can't see it when you're inside!
6 My bedroom is my favorite room. It has big windows, and it's really _____ all day.

◀ Go back to page 84

152

VOCABULARY PRACTICE

10B Describing appearance

1 ▶ 10.6 Complete the diagrams with the words in the box. Listen and check.

| curly | earrings | elderly | light | gray | heavy | medium-length | mustache | slim | tall |

2 Match pictures a–h with the descriptions.

1 This person is elderly. She has wavy gray hair. _____
2 This person has short brown hair. He doesn't have an earring. _____
3 This person is young. She has medium-length red hair. _____
4 This person has medium-length light hair. She wears glasses. _____
5 This person has short blond hair, a beard, and a moustache. He doesn't wear glasses. _____
6 This person is bald, with a white beard, and mustache. He wears glasses. _____
7 This person has black hair. She has black earrings. _____
8 This person is middle-aged. He has brown hair and an earring. _____

◀ Go back to page 86

VOCABULARY PRACTICE

10C Personality adjectives

1 ▶ 10.10 Match the adjectives in the box with pictures 1–12. Listen and check.

| smart confident funny generous kind popular lazy polite brave cheerful shy talkative |

1 _____

2 _____

3 _____

4 _____

5 _____

6 _____

7 _____

8 _____

9 _____

10 _____

11 _____

12 _____

2 Choose the correct adjectives to complete the sentences.
1 My brother hates parties because he's really *generous / shy*.
2 Elvira is very *talkative / polite* in class. The teacher sometimes says, "Please be quiet for a moment, Elvira!"
3 Jürgen was really *smart / kind* to me after I failed my exam.
4 Sam is *confident / nice* when she speaks English. She always wants to practice.
5 I want to lose weight. I need to be a little less *lazy / brave* and get more exercise!
6 I think it's important to be *polite / funny*, so I always say "please" and "thank you."

3 Complete the sentences with words from exercise 1.
1 Alison is very _____. She always pays for my coffee.
2 Joe is so _____. He makes everyone laugh.
3 I wish I was _____ like my friend. He always gets good grades.
4 Most people are _____, although there are some horrible people.
5 You're so _____! Are you really going to do a bungee jump?
6 Belinda is always _____, even when things aren't going well for her.

◀ Go back to page 88

154

VOCABULARY PRACTICE

11A Travel and transportation

1 ▶ 11.1 Complete expressions 1–18 with the words in the box.

| bike   boat   bus (x2)   car   ferry   foot   helicopter   motorcycle |
| plane   scooter   ship   streetcar   subway   taxi   train   truck   van |

 1 by _____

 2 by _____

 3 by _____

 4 by _____

 5 by _____

 6 by _____

 7 by _____

 8 on _____

 9 by _____

 10 by _____

 11 by _____

 12 by _____

 13 by _____

 14 by _____

 15 by _____

 16 by _____

 17 by _____

 18 by _____

2 Write the forms of transportation in the correct columns.

by water	by air	on land

3 Choose the correct phrases to complete the sentences.
1 I prefer to go to work *by bike / by bus*. The exercise wakes me up.
2 I'm scared of flying, so I wouldn't want to go *by helicopter / by motorcycle*.
3 I don't like to take the subway after midnight, so I usually go home *by ship / by taxi* if I'm out late.
4 A lot of people travel *by ferry / by motorcycle* in my city. It's quicker and easier than by car.
5 I love traveling *by car / by train*. You can walk around, if you want!
6 I go to college *by subway / by van*. I can't sightsee, but it's very quick.
7 I'm from France, but I live in Spain. I usually go home to visit my family *by bus / by truck*. It's sometimes slower, but it's cheaper than flying.
8 My town is next to a very wide river. There's no bridge, but you can go across the river *by streetcar / by ferry*.

155   ◀ Go back to page 94

VOCABULARY PRACTICE

11C Vacation activities

1 ▶ 11.5 Match sentences 1–12 with pictures a–l.

1 They're going sightseeing. ____
2 She's going surfing. ____
3 They're going to the beach. ____
4 They're going to the mountains. ____
5 She's going hiking. ____
6 She's relaxing on the beach. ____
7 He's relaxing by the pool. ____
8 They're staying at a hotel. ____
9 She's staying at an apartment. ____
10 They're staying at a campsite. ____
11 She's staying with friends. ____
12 They're visiting a museum/an art gallery. ____

 a
 b
 c
 d
 e
 f
 g
 h
 i
 j
 k
 l

2 Read about the people. Then choose a vacation activity from the box for them.

| a stay at an apartment | c go surfing | e stay at a campsite | g visit a museum/an art gallery |
| b go hiking | d relax by the pool | f go sightseeing | h stay at a hotel |

1 Luís likes walking in different places, like mountains and forests. ____
2 Shelley and Phil like visiting cities, but they don't like staying at hotels. ____
3 Juan is very athletic, and he loves the ocean. ____
4 Hong likes art and history. ____
5 Maciek doesn't like doing housework like cooking and making the bed. He likes staying at very comfortable places. ____
6 Linus loves visiting cities. He always wants to see a lot of different places and take lots of photos. ____
7 Fabio has three new books to read. He loves hot weather, but he doesn't like the sea. ____
8 Mina and her family love the country. They like being outside, and they don't like hotels. ____

◀ Go back to page 98

VOCABULARY PRACTICE

12A Entertainment

1 ▶ 12.1 Match the people in the box with pictures 1–6 and the events with pictures 7–12. Listen and check.

| actor   artist   dancer   band/musician   opera singer   player |

| concert   game   opera   play   exhibit   ballet |

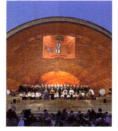

1 _____   2 _____   3 _____   7 _____   8 _____   9 _____

4 _____   5 _____   6 _____   10 _____   11 _____   12 _____

2 Complete the chart with words from exercise 1.

person/people	event
1 _____	exhibit
band	2 _____
3 _____	ballet
4 _____	game
actor	5 _____
singer	6 _____

3 Complete the sentences with words from exercise 1.
1 I love this _____'s work. She uses beautiful colors.
2 My friend's _____ are really good. They play rock music.
3 Do you like _____? Or do you prefer modern dance?
4 How many _____ are there on a soccer team?
5 What's your favorite Shakespeare _____?
6 There's an art _____ at City Hall.
7 Did you go to the jazz _____ on Friday night?
8 My cousin is an _____. He's been on TV a few times.

◀ Go back to page 102

12B Opinion adjectives

1 ▶ 12.6 Complete the chart with the adjectives in the box. Listen and check.

| awesome   awful   boring   amazing   exciting   interesting
all right   terrible   sad   strange   horrible   fun   fantastic
stupid   cool   great   scary |

Positive ☺	OK 😐	Negative ☹

2 Read the sentences and choose the adjective that's not possible.
1 This play is *terrible / cool / boring*. Can we go home now?
2 I don't like *sad / scary / exciting* movies. I prefer action movies.
3 I had an amazing time at the party last night. It was *all right / awesome / fun*.
4 New York is a really *interesting / exciting / scary* city. I'm going to go there again.
5 We had a nice vacation in Chile, but the weather was *awful / horrible / great*.
6 I don't think I like Pedro very much. He's a bit *fun / strange / scary*!
7 I went to hear a really *fantastic / awesome / terrible* singer on the weekend. She was amazing!
8 The movie was a bit *interesting / stupid / strange*. I didn't really like it.

◀ Go back to page 104

157

COMMUNICATION PRACTICE

7A Student A

1. Look at the two recipes. Ask Student B if he/she has the food items. Which dish can you cook?

   A *Do you have any eggs?*
   B *Yes. I have six.*

   <u>Omelet</u>
   3 eggs
   1 onion
   potatoes
   1 pepper
   cheese

   <u>Stirfry</u>
   rice
   2 peppers
   2 carrots
   2 onions
   chicken

2. Look at the food in your kitchen. Answer Student B's questions.

   B *Do you have any beef?*
   A *Yes, I do.*

162

COMMUNICATION PRACTICE

7C Student A

1. Read about the Mediterranean diet. Ask Student B about the food items in the box and complete the sentences.

   A *Can you eat any cheese on the Mediterranean diet?*
   B *Yes, but you can't eat much.*

cheese	fish	lemons	onions	olive oil	pastries
tomatoes	meat	eggs	oranges	candy	

   ### THE MEDITERRANEAN DIET

   People who live near the Mediterranean Sea usually live for a long time and are healthy. If you want to try the Mediterranean diet, follow these rules:

   You can eat a lot of: _____.

   You can't eat much/many: _____.

   You can't eat any: _____.

2. Read about the Paleo diet. Look at the pictures and answer Student B's questions.

   B *Can you eat any bananas on the Paleo diet?*
   A *Yes, but you can't eat many.*

   ### THE PALEO DIET

   The Paleo diet is similar to what people ate 2.5 million years ago. You can only eat natural food. If you want to try the Paleo diet, follow these rules:

   You can eat a lot of:

   You can't eat much/many:

   You can't eat/drink any:

7D Student A

1. You are a waiter. Read each sentence to your partner and wait for his/her response. Read the next sentence. Sentences 1 and 2 are on the telephone.

   1. *Good afternoon, The Red Lion Restaurant. How can I help?*
   2. *For how many people?*
   3. *Hello. How can I help you?*
   4. *Are you ready to order?*
   5. *Would you like a starter?*
   6. *And what would you like for the main course?*
   7. *Would you like that with French fries or salad?*
   8. *Can I get you any drinks?*
   9. *Would you like anything for dessert?*

2. Now switch roles and repeat the activity. You are Student B. Go to page 172.

8A Student A

1. Read the facts for each decade to Student B. Don't say the decade! Ask him/her to guess the decade.

2. Now listen to Student B's facts. Try to guess the decade.

   Is it the nineteen eighties?
   Is it the two thousands?

GUESS THE DECADE!

In this decade ...
- people had black-and-white TVs.
- the Russians sent the first satellite into space.
- John Wayne, Frank Sinatra, and Marilyn Monroe were popular Hollywood stars.

Answer: the 1950s ("nineteen fifties")

In this decade ...
- the Summer Olympics were in China.
- some countries in Europe had a new type of money.
- a lot of people bought a GPS.

Answer: the 2000s ("two thousands")

8C Student A

1. Look at the information in the chart. Take turns telling Student B facts about the people, using the simple past. Listen and complete the chart with Student B's information.

   A *Paulo was born in Recife, in Brazil.*

2. Compare your information with Student B. Is it the same?

	Paulo	Emma	Daria
be born in	Recife, in Brazil		St. Petersburg, in Russia
want to be / when he/she / be / a child		a pilot	
study / in college	French		medicine
travel to		Peru in 2015	
cook / for dinner last night	lasagna		steak
play		chess on the weekend	

COMMUNICATION PRACTICE

9A Student A

Ask Student B simple past questions to complete the text about Fabia's elementary school. Answer Student B's questions.

A *Where was Fabia's school?*
B *It was one mile from her house.*

Finland has one of the best education systems in the world. Read about Fabia's time in elementary school.

I didn't go to nursery school or kindergarten. I started elementary school when I was seven years old. My school was [1]_____ (where?). I went to school by bus every day.
I [2]_____ school (did / enjoy?)! Classes started at nine o'clock in the morning. There were fifteen students in my class, and I always sat next to [3]_____ (who?). My teacher's name was Johannes, and he was our teacher for six years. My favorite subjects were [4]_____ (what?), and I still love learning foreign languages now. I hated math, and I was bad at [5]_____ (what subjects?).

9C Student A

Take turns reading the sentences with Student B. Student B finishes your sentences and you finish Student B's sentences.

	Your sentences	Student B's sentences
1	Jenna is studying Spanish. She's planning ...	... to save some money every month.
2	Saul wants to be a doctor. He needs ...	... to spend some time in the U.S. to improve it.
3	Carlotta eats a lot of junk food. She wants ...	... to improve their relationship.
4	Hans wants to lose weight. He'd like ...	... to do a course in Asian cooking.
5	Brigit doesn't like her job. She's hoping ...	... to learn to write computer programs.
6	Sasha moved to a new city recently. She'd like ...	... to get in shape this year.

9D Student A

1 Read your problems to Student B. Listen to his/her suggestion(s) and respond.

  A *I left my backpack on the bus this morning!*
  B *How terrible! Can you call the Lost and Found?*
  A *That's a good idea.*

  - I left my backpack on the bus this morning!
  - I have an exam tomorrow, but I don't know the subject very well.
  - I can't study at home because it's always noisy.
  - My roommate never cleans the kitchen.
  - My laptop stopped working last night!

2 Listen to Student B's problems. Sound sympathetic and make suggestions to him/her from the list below.

  B *My boss lives in New York, and she only visits us once a year.*
  A *I'm sure it's difficult to be so far away from her. How about asking her to visit twice a year?*
  B *I'm not sure I should. She's very busy.*

  - take some time off work and visit her
  - watch less television in the evening
  - ask your boss to visit twice a year
  - get more practice and take it again
  - turn your phone off

164

COMMUNICATION PRACTICE

10A Student A

1. You want to reserve a hotel for your vacation. You have two young children. Ask Student B questions to find out about the two hotels. Which one is better?

   A *Which hotel is nearer the beach?*
   B *The Apex Hotel is nearer the beach.*

   You're looking for a hotel that is:

	APEX HOTEL	SEA VIEW HOTEL
near the beach	☐	☐
quiet	☐	☐
small	☐	☐
friendly	☐	☐
clean	☐	☐
safe	☐	☐
less expensive	☐	☐

2. You are a travel agent. Answer Student B's questions about the two hotels.

	Sunset Hotel	Party Hotel
Price	$$$	$
Beach	100 meters	600 meters
Clubs	300 meters	10 meters
Stores	50 meters	1 kilometer
Number of rooms	60	200
Comments	modern hotel (2015) uncomfortable beds cheap food	old hotel (1970) comfortable beds expensive food

10C Student A

Take turns asking and answer the trivia questions with Student B. You have different questions. Complete the questions with the superlative of the adjectives in parentheses. Score 1 point for each correct answer. Who can score the most points? The correct answers are in red. Tell Student B the extra information about the correct answers.

A *What is the cleanest city in the world? a) Calgary in Canada, b) Tokyo in Japan, or c) Florence in Italy?*

GENERAL KNOWLEDGE TRIVIA

1. What is _____ (clean) city in the world?   a) **Calgary in Canada**   b) Tokyo in Japan   c) Florence in Italy
   In a 2016 survey, Calgary in Canada was the winner of "The Cleanest City" award.

2. Who was _____ (popular) person on Facebook in 2016?   a) Daniel Radcliffe   b) **Cristiano Ronaldo**   c) Meryl Streep
   In 2016, Cristiano Ronaldo had more than 107 million "Likes" on Facebook.

3. How long was _____ (long) pizza in the world?   a) 800 meters   b) **1.8 kilometers**   c) 80 meters
   In 2016, 250 pizza chefs made a pizza that was 1.8 kilometers long in Naples, Italy. They used 2,000 kilograms of mozzarella cheese.

4. What soccer team has _____ (noisy) fans in the world?   a) Arsenal in England   b) Colo Colo in Chile   c) **Galatasaray in Turkey**
   The noise of Galatasaray fans at their stadium in Istanbul can reach 130 decibels – that's louder than a jet airplane when it takes off!

5. What is _____ (high) capital city in the world?   a) **La Paz in Bolivia**   b) Addis Ababa in Ethiopia   c) Kathmandu in Nepal
   La Paz in Bolivia is 3,640 meters above sea level. For tourists, it can be hard to breathe, walk, and sleep.

11A Student A

1. Ask Student B questions about John's job, using *have to*. Complete the chart with *yes* or *no*. Then guess what John's job is.

   A *Does John have to wear a uniform at work?*
   B *No, he doesn't.*

2. Now answer Student B's questions about Tiffany. You can only say *yes* or *no*.

	JOHN	TIFFANY
		Tiffany is a flight attendant.
1 wear a uniform?		Yes
2 drive at work?		No
3 work at night sometimes?		Yes
4 travel to other countries?		Yes
5 help people?		Yes
6 be in shape?		Yes
7 work alone?		No
8 speak to a lot of people?		Yes

COMMUNICATION PRACTICE

11C Student A

1 Ask Student B about his/her vacation plans and complete the chart. Use *be going to*.

A *Where are you going to go?*
B *I'm going to go to Lima in Peru.*

2 Now answer Student B's questions about your vacation plans. Use the information in the chart.

		You	Student B
1	Where / go?	Crete, Greece	
2	When / go?	June 10th	
3	Who / go with?	my family	
4	How / travel?	boat	
5	Where / stay?	apartment	
6	What / do?	relax by the pool go to the beach play tennis go surfing	
7	When / return?	June 24th	

11D Student A

1 You are Karol. You are checking in at the Sea View Hotel. Tell the receptionist about your reservation, answer his/her questions, and ask for the missing information. Check anything that you aren't sure about.

Your name	Karol Lisicki
Type of room	Deluxe room
Number of nights	2
Discount?	?
Breakfast included?	?
WiFi password	?
Room number and floor	?

B *Welcome to the Sea View Hotel. Checking in?*
A *Yes. I reserved a room in the name of …*

2 You are the receptionist at the Castle Hotel. Greet the guest, ask for his/her reservation information, and give him/her the information he/she asks for.

Guest name	?
Type of room	?
Number of nights	?
Discount?	NO
Breakfast included?	YES
WiFi password	THECASTLE99
Room number and floor	357, third floor

12A Student A

1 Ask and answer questions with Student B about the people in the chart. Use the present perfect + *ever*.

A *Has Henry ever been to a music festival?*   B *Yes, he has.*

	Nadia	Henry	Elena	Oliver
go to a music festival	✗			✓
watch a basketball game		✗	✓	
see the Mona Lisa in Paris			✓	✗
travel to another continent	✓	✗		
climb a mountain		✗	✗	
study a foreign language	✗			✗
dance all night			✓	✗
sing in a band	✓	✗		

2 Now imagine that you work for a dating agency. Work with Student B. Which two of the four people have the most similar interests?

12C Student A

1 Ask Student B questions with the prompts. Use the present perfect + *ever* for question "a," and the simple past for question "b." Then decide if you think his/her answer is true.

A *Have you ever met a famous person?*
B *Yes, I have.*
A *Who did you meet?*
B *I met Penélope Cruz.*
A *I think that's true.*
B *No, it's not true!*

a you / meet a famous person?   b Who / you / meet?
a you / win a competition?   b What / you / win?
a you / buy / flowers for someone?   b Who / you / buy them for?
a you / be / the U.S.?   b Which cities / you / visit?
a you / see / the same movie several times? b Which movie / be / it?
a you / eat / sushi?   b What / you think of it?

2 Now answer Student B's questions. For question "a," answer *Yes, I have*. Invent information for each question "b," if necessary.

166

COMMUNICATION PRACTICE

7A Student B

1. Look at the food in your kitchen. Answer Student A's questions.

   A *Do you have any eggs?*
   B *Yes. I have six.*

2. Look at the two recipes. Ask Student A if he/she has the food items. Which dish can you cook?

   B *Do you have any beef?*
   A *Yes, I do.*

<u>Kebab</u>
beef
1 onion
bread
yogurt
2 peppers

<u>Spaghetti Bolognese</u>
beef
1 onion
3 tomatoes
spaghetti
1 pepper

COMMUNICATION PRACTICE

7C Student B

1 Read about the Mediterranean diet. Look at the pictures and answer Student A's questions.

   A *Can you eat any cheese on the Mediterranean diet?*
   B *Yes, but you can't eat much.*

   ### THE MEDITERRANEAN DIET
   People who live near the Mediterranean Sea usually live for a long time and are healthy. If you want to try the Mediterranean diet, follow these rules:

   You can eat a lot of:

   You can't eat much/many:

   You can't eat any:

2 Read about the Paleo diet. Ask Student A about the food items in the box and complete the sentences.

   B *Can you eat any bananas on the Paleo diet?*
   A *Yes, but you can't eat many.*

   | bananas | apples | milk | nuts | fish | meat |
   | bread | eggs | potatoes | coffee | cheese |

   ### THE PALEO DIET
   The Paleo diet is similar to what people ate 2.5 million years ago. You can only eat natural food. If you want to try the Paleo diet, follow these rules:

   You can eat/drink a lot of: _____.

   You can't eat/drink much/many: _____.

   You can't eat/drink any: _____.

7D Student B

1 You are a restaurant customer. Listen to your partner. Choose a sentence and answer.

   1 It's for six people.
   2 Yes. Can I have the chicken soup, please?
   3 Yes. Could I have some seltzer, please?
   4 With French fries, please.
   5 I'd like to reserve a table for Wednesday evening, please.
   6 Hello. We have a table reserved in the name of Cox.
   7 I'd like the steak, please.
   8 No, thank you. Could we have the check, please?
   9 Yes, we are.

2 Now switch roles and repeat the activity. You are Student A. Go to page 163.

8A Student B

1 Listen to Student A's facts. Try to guess the decade.

   Is it the nineteen sixties?
   Is it the nineteen thirties?

2 Now read the facts for each decade to Student A. Don't say the decade! Ask him/her to guess the decade.

GUESS THE DECADE!

In this decade ...
- Space Invaders and Pac-Man were popular video games.
- people first bought cell phones in stores.
- the UK had its first female Prime Minister.

Answer: the 1980s ("nineteen eighties")

In this decade ...
- the first Winter Olympics were in France.
- jazz music was popular.
- there was a new country – the USSR.

Answer: the 1920s ("nineteen twenties")

8C Student B

1 Look at the information in the chart. Take turns telling Student A facts about the people, using the simple past. Listen and complete the chart with Student A's information.

   B *Emma was born in Austin, in the U.S.*

2 Compare your information with Student A. Is it the same?

	Paulo	Emma	Daria
be born in		Austin, in the U.S.	
want to be / when he/she / be / a child	a chef		a doctor
study / in college		history	
travel to	China in 2007		Canada in 1998
cook / for dinner last night		spaghetti	
play	golf on the weekend		volleyball yesterday afternoon

172

COMMUNICATION PRACTICE

9A Student B

Ask Student A simple past questions to complete the text about Fabia's elementary school. Answer Student A's questions.

B *Did Fabia go to nursery school and kindergarten?*
A *No, she didn't.*

Finland has one of the best education systems in the world. Read about Fabia's time in elementary school.

I ¹_____ (did / go?) to nursery school or kindergarten. I started elementary school when I was seven years old. My school was one mile from my house. I went to school ²_____ (how?) every day. I really enjoyed school! Classes started at ³_____ (what time?). There were fifteen students in my class, and I always sat next to my best friend, Emma. My teacher's name was ⁴_____ (what?), and he was our teacher for six years. My favorite subjects were English and Swedish, and I still love learning foreign languages now. I hated ⁵_____ (what subject?), and I was bad at art and music.

9C Student B

Take turns reading the sentences with Student A. Student A finishes your sentences and you finish Student A's sentences.

	Your sentences	Student A's sentences
1	Kyle and his girlfriend argue a lot. They need …	… to improve her diet.
2	Christa is joining a gym. She's hoping …	… to travel through South America.
3	Mahmood is interested in IT. He'd like …	… to start running.
4	Eleni's English isn't very good. She's planning …	… to make some new friends.
5	Nathan loves Thai food. He wants …	… to get a new job soon.
6	Claire wants to buy a new car. She's hoping …	… to get a place to study medicine in college.

9D Student B

1 Listen to Student A's problems. Sound sympathetic and make suggestions for him/her from the list below.

A *I left my backpack on the bus this morning!*
B *How terrible! Can you call the Lost and Found?*
A *That's a good idea.*

- go to the library
- take it to the repair shop
- call the Lost and Found
- watch some online videos about your subject
- talk to him/her about it

2 Read your problems to Student A. Listen to his/her suggestion(s) and respond.

B *My boss lives in New York, and she only visits us once a year.*
A *I'm sure it's difficult to be so far away from her. How about asking her to visit twice a year?*
B *I'm not sure I should. She's very busy.*

- My boss lives in New York, and she only visits us once a year.
- I failed my driving test yesterday.
- My mother's in the hospital, but I'm very busy at work.
- My friends call me in the evening when I want to study.
- I often don't have time to do my homework in the evening.

COMMUNICATION PRACTICE

10A Student B

1 You are a travel agent. Answer Student A's questions about the two hotels.

   A *Which hotel is nearer the beach?*
   B *The Apex Hotel is nearer the beach.*

	Apex Hotel	Sea View Hotel
Price	$$	$$$
Beach	200 meters	500 meters
Clubs	30 meters	1 kilometer
Stores	100 meters	2 kilometers
Number of rooms	80	20
Comments	friendly staff dirty rooms on a busy street	unfriendly staff clean rooms safe, quiet location

2 You want to reserve a hotel for your vacation. You're going on vacation with a big group of friends. Ask Student A questions to find out about the two hotels. Which one is better?

You're looking for a hotel that is:

	SUNSET HOTEL	PARTY HOTEL
near the beach	☐	☐
near the clubs	☐	☐
good for shopping	☐	☐
big	☐	☐
modern	☐	☐
comfortable	☐	☐
cheap	☐	☐

10C Student B

Take turns asking and answering the trivia questions with Student A. You both have different questions. Complete the questions with the superlative of the adjectives in parentheses. Score 1 point for each correct answer. Who can score the most points? The correct answers are in red. Tell Student A the extra information about the correct answers.

   A *What is the happiest country in the world? a) Brazil, b) Australia or c) Denmark?*

GENERAL KNOWLEDGE TRIVIA

1 **According to a UN report, what is _____ (happy) country in the world?**   a) Brazil   b) Australia   c) **Denmark**
   With a population of 5.6 million, Denmark reached Number 1 in the "World Happiness Report" in 2016.

2 **Which was _____ (expensive) film of these three?**   a) **Pirates of the Caribbean 4**   b) Titanic   c) Jurassic World
   Pirates of the Caribbean 4 cost $378.5 million in 2011. It didn't get good reviews, but it earned more than $1 billion.

3 **How big is _____ (big) spider in the world?**   a) **30 centimeters wide**   b) 1 meter wide   c) 10 centimeters wide
   The Goliath Birdeater tarantula lives in the rainforests of South America and is the size of a dinner plate!

4 **Which is _____ (cheap) car in the world?**   a) Lamborghini Aventador   b) **Tata Nano**   c) Volkswagen Golf
   The Tata Nano is made in India. It cost $2,000 in 2009.

5 **How tall was _____ (tall) man in the world?**   a) 3.24 meters   b) 2.43 meters   c) **2.72 meters**
   Robert Wadlow was born in 1918 in the U.S. In 1940, he was 2.72 meters tall.

11A Student B

1 Answer Student A's questions about John's job. You can only say *yes* or *no*.

   A *Does John have to wear a uniform at work?*
   B *No, he doesn't.*

2 Now ask Student A questions about Tiffany's job, using *have to*. Complete the chart with *yes* or *no*. Then guess what Tiffany's job is.

	JOHN	TIFFANY
	John is a truck driver.	
1 wear a uniform?	No	
2 drive at work?	Yes	
3 work at night sometimes?	Yes	
4 travel to other countries?	Yes	
5 help people?	No	
6 be in shape?	No	
7 work alone?	Yes	
8 speak to a lot of people?	No	

174

COMMUNICATION PRACTICE

11C Student B

1. Answer Student A's questions about your vacation plans. Use the information in the chart.

   A *Where are you going to go?*
   B *I'm going to go to Lima in Peru.*

2. Now ask Student A about his/her vacation plans and complete the chart. Use *be going to*.

	Student A	You
1	Where / go?	Lima, Peru
2	When / go?	January 16th
3	Who / go with?	my partner
4	How / travel?	plane
5	Where / stay?	hotel
6	What / do?	try local food
		visit the museums
		go shopping
		watch a soccer game
7	When / return?	January 30th

11D Student B

1. You are the receptionist at the Sea View Hotel. Greet the guest, ask for his/her reservation information, and give him/her the information he/she asks for.

Guest name	?
Type of room	?
Number of nights	?
Discount?	YES
Breakfast included?	NO
WiFi password	seaviewhotel2000
Room number and floor	105, first floor

   B *Welcome to the Sea View Hotel. Checking in?*
   A *Yes. I reserved a room in the name of …*

2. You are Wendy. You are checking in at the Castle Hotel. Tell the receptionist about your reservation, answer his/her questions, and ask for the missing information. Check anything that you're not sure about.

Your name	Wendy Zhao
Type of room	Standard room
Number of nights	3
Discount?	?
Breakfast included?	?
WiFi password	?
Room number and floor	?

12A Student B

1. Ask and answer questions with Student A about the people in the chart. Use the present perfect + *ever*.

   B *Has Nadia ever been to a music festival?* A *No, she hasn't.*

	Nadia	Henry	Elena	Oliver
go to a music festival		✔	✘	
watch a basketball game	✔			✔
see the Mona Lisa in Paris	✘	✔		
travel to another continent	✔		✘	✔
climb a mountain	✔			✔
study a foreign language		✔	✔	
dance all night	✔	✔		
sing in a band			✘	✔

2. Now imagine that you work for a dating agency. Work with Student A. Which two of the four people have the most similar interests?

12C Student B

1. Answer Student A's questions. For question "a," answer *Yes, I have*. Invent information for each question "b" if necessary.

2. Now ask Student A questions with the prompts. Use the present perfect + *ever* for question "a," and the simple past for question "b." Then decide if you think his/her answer is true.

   A *Have you ever lost something important?*
   B *Yes, I have.*
   A *What did you lose?*
   B *I lost my credit card.*
   A *I think that's true.*
   B *No, it's not true!*

   a you / lost something important? b What / you / lose?
   a you / fly / in a helicopter? b Where / you / go?
   a you / see / a lion? b Where / you / see it?
   a you / go / the UK? b Which cities / you / visit?
   a you / read / the same book several times? b Which book / be / it?
   a you / eat / curry? b What / you think of it?

175

IRREGULAR VERBS

Infinitive	Past simple	Past participle
be	was, were	been
become	became	become
begin	began	begun
bite	bit	bitten
break	broke	broken
bring	brought	brought
build	built	built
buy	bought	bought
choose	chose	chosen
come	came	come
cost	cost	cost
do	did	done
forbid	forbade	forbidden
forget	forgot	forgotten
forgive	forgave	forgiven
get	got	gotten
give	gave	given
go	went	gone
grow	grew	grown
have	had	had
hear	heard	heard
hide	hid	hidden
hold	held	held
keep	kept	kept
know	knew	known
leave	left	left
let	let	let
lose	lost	lost
make	made	made

Infinitive	Past simple	Past participle
meet	met	met
pay	paid	paid
put	put	put
read (/riːd/)	read (/red/)	read (/red/)
ride	rode	ridden
ring	rang	rung
rise	rose	risen
run	ran	run
say	said	said
see	saw	seen
sell	sold	sold
send	sent	sent
sleep	slept	slept
speak	spoke	spoken
spend	spent	spent
stand	stood	stood
steal	stole	stolen
stick	stuck	stuck
swim	swam	swum
take	took	taken
teach	taught	taught
tell	told	told
think	thought	thought
throw	threw	thrown
understand	understood	understood
wake	woke	woken
wear	wore	worn
win	won	won
write	wrote	written

American English

Personal Best

Workbook

A2
Elementary

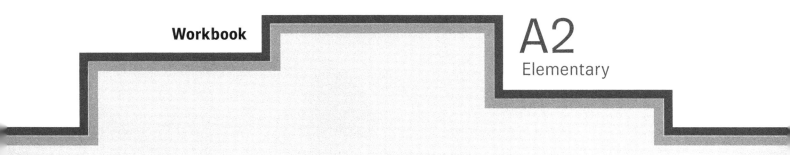

UNIT 7 Food and drink

7A LANGUAGE

GRAMMAR: Countable and uncountable nouns + *some/any*

1 Are the nouns countable (C) or uncountable (U)?

1 cheese	C U	6 jewelry	C U
2 salt	C U	7 teacher	C U
3 library	C U	8 mirror	C U
4 bread	C U	9 pasta	C U
5 lemonade	C U	10 sofa	C U

2 Complete the sentences with *some* or *any*.

1 Is there _____ coffee in the cabinet?
2 I'd like _____ yogurt.
3 There isn't _____ tea here – can you buy some?
4 Can I have _____ onions? I need them to make lunch.
5 She usually has _____ fruit after dinner.
6 Would you like _____ tomato soup?
7 Are there _____ lemons in the kitchen?
8 I don't want _____ water.

VOCABULARY: Food and drink

3 Complete the conversation with the words in the box. There are two extra words.

juice   ice cream   cookies   tea   potatoes
cake   peas   cereal   orange   mushroom

Miguel Peter's coming to dinner tonight.
Eva Great! I can make some
¹_____ soup. I know he likes it.
Miguel We have some fish. Do we have any
²_____? I can make some French fries. We can have some
³_____, too.
Eva That sounds good! What about drinks? Do we need any ⁴_____?
Miguel Yes, Peter's favorite is
⁵_____.
Eva OK. Now we need something for dessert. ⁶_____?
Miguel No, it's too cold! Why don't you get a
⁷_____?
Eva Great idea! And after that, we can have
⁸_____ or coffee.

4 Write the words for definitions 1–8. Then match 1–8 with pictures a–h.

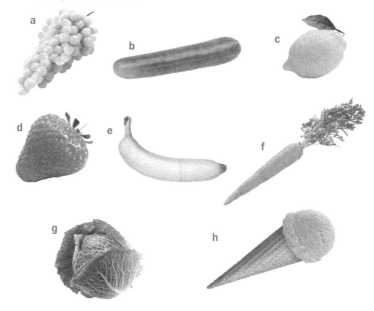

1 a long green vegetable   c_____
2 a small round red fruit   s_____
3 you eat this in hot weather   i____ c_____
4 a long yellow fruit   b_____
5 a long orange vegetable   c_____
6 a large round green vegetable   c_____
7 a small round fruit, sometimes green   g_____
8 a round yellow fruit   l_____

PRONUNCIATION: *some/any*

5 ▶ 7.1 Say the sentences. Are *some* and *any* stressed? Listen, check, and repeat.

1 There are some bananas on the table.
2 Is there any milk in the fridge?
3 She's buying some strawberries at the market.
4 I don't want any cookies, thanks.
5 There isn't any pepper.
6 I'd like some potato chips with my lunch.

SKILLS 7B

READING: Skimming a text

BREAKFAST AROUND THE WORLD!

Breakfast is the most important meal of the day because it gives us the energy we need to work and learn. In many European countries, the first meal of the day is a piece of bread and some coffee. In other countries, people eat much more. So, what exactly do people around the world have for breakfast?

Paulo, Brazil:
I have breakfast with my family – we sit together and talk about the day ahead. We usually have coffee and some bread with cheese. We also like to have some fruit – it's delicious!

Jason, Australia:
In Australia, we have lots of excellent seasonal fruit, so it's a popular breakfast. I'm too busy to cook in the morning, so I often have an apple and some yogurt. Sometimes I don't even have enough time to eat that, so I take the yogurt to work with me.

Jenny, Ireland:
I leave home early, so I rarely eat anything. I usually just have a cup of tea. I know it's really unhealthy! On weekends, I have more time – so I have an egg sandwich.

Asil, Turkey:
My mom always makes my breakfast – she's an excellent cook. I usually have some bread, cheese, eggs, and tomatoes – that's a popular breakfast in Turkey.

Yoko, Japan:
For breakfast, I often have rice and vegetables. I like miso soup, too. It is a very popular breakfast in Japan. I sometimes have that because it's a healthy breakfast. It gives me energy to study when I'm in school.

1 Skim the text. Answer the questions with one word.
1 Many European people drink coffee for _____.
2 Brazilians often have bread with _____.
3 _____ is a popular breakfast in Australia.
4 Jenny usually has a cup of _____ for breakfast.
5 Asil's _____ is a really good cook.
6 People in _____ eat miso soup.

2 Choose the correct options to answer the questions.
1 Breakfast is important because
  a it gives you energy for the day.
  b you eat it with your family.
  c it helps you sleep better.
2 Paulo eats his first meal of the day
  a alone.
  b with his family.
  c with his friends.
3 Why doesn't Jenny eat breakfast?
  a She thinks it's unhealthy.
  b She's too busy.
  c She doesn't have enough money.
4 Jenny eats egg sandwiches
  a for lunch.
  b on Saturdays and Sundays.
  c every day.
5 In Turkey, a lot of people
  a don't eat breakfast.
  b eat the same breakfast as Asil.
  c drink tea for breakfast.
6 Yoko
  a has breakfast in school.
  b rarely eats miso soup.
  c doesn't eat the same breakfast every day.

3 Choose the correct options to complete the sentences.
1 Paulo eats breakfast with his family. *He / They / We* sit and talk about the day ahead.
2 Jason doesn't have time to eat breakfast. *His / Its / Their* morning is just too busy!
3 I love eggs. *It's / My / Their* favorite breakfast is an egg sandwich.
4 Fruit is really good in Australia. *Its / It's / It* a popular breakfast.
5 Asil's mother makes his breakfast. *She / Her / He* is an excellent cook.
6 Yoko thinks breakfast is important. *They / It / She* gives her energy to study when she's in school.
7 Most of us eat breakfast, but *you / we / it* eat different things in different countries.
8 We usually go out for lunch on a Sunday. *Your / Its / Our* favorite restaurant is Gino's.

7C LANGUAGE

GRAMMAR: Quantifiers: *(how) much*, *(how) many*, *a lot of*, *a few*, *a little*

1 Choose the correct options to complete the sentences.

1 I'm drinking _____ carrot juice right now. I want to be healthy.
   a much   b a lot of   c a few
2 Can I have _____ milk in my coffee, please?
   a many   b a few   c a little
3 How _____ meals do you usually eat?
   a many   b much   c few
4 Sara eats _____ cakes and cookies. It's not very healthy!
   a a little   b a few   c a lot of
5 "Are there any potatoes?" "There are _____."
   a a few   b a little   c much
6 Millie usually has _____ cereal for breakfast, but I don't think it's enough.
   a a little   b a lot of   c many
7 How _____ meat does he eat every week?
   a much   b little   c many

2 Complete the text with the correct quantifiers. Write one word in each space.

People often ask me how to stay healthy. I have a ¹_____ good ideas. First, I always have a big breakfast, so I don't need ²_____ snacks in the middle of the morning. The people I work with eat a lot ³_____ cakes and cookies at eleven o'clock – not me! I eat ⁴_____ little cake sometimes and a ⁵_____ potato chips – but not many. How ⁶_____ cola do I drink? None! I drink a ⁷_____ coffee, but I drink a ⁸_____ of water, too. And how ⁹_____ glasses of water do I drink? Probably about seven every day.

VOCABULARY: Containers and portions

3 Match the two parts of the sentences.

1 Could we have a can _____
2 I need a bottle of _____
3 Can you buy a box _____
4 He'd like a bag of _____
5 Is there a bag of _____
6 Laura has a bar _____
7 I often have a bowl _____

a of chocolate in her desk.
b water – I'm really thirsty!
c of pasta for my dinner.
d potato chips with his lunch.
e of corn, please?
f onions in the kitchen?
g of cereal for breakfast tomorrow?

4 Complete the words.

1 I'm going to the store for a c_____ of milk.
2 "There are no fresh tomatoes." "Why don't you buy some in a c_____?"
3 It's my birthday today! Have a s_____ of cake.
4 My mom has a c_____ of tea every morning.
5 It's really hot! Do you want a g_____ of cold water?
6 There are some olives in that j_____. Would you like some?
7 Have a p_____ of this cheese with your bread.

PRONUNCIATION: Weak form *of*

5 ▶7.2 Say the sentences. How do we say *of*? Listen, check, and repeat.

1 I don't eat a lot of candy.
2 How many cups of coffee do you drink?
3 Do you want a box of cookies?
4 How many glasses of juice do they want?
5 There is a bowl of fruit on the table.
6 Where is the bottle of olive oil?

SKILLS 7D

SPEAKING: Asking politely for something

1 ▶ 7.3 Listen. What do the customers order at the restaurant? Choose the correct information.

1	2	3	4
3 customers Name: Cellini 2 x vegetable soup 1 x steak + French fries 1 x lasagna 2 x mineral water 2 x fruit salad	2 customers Name: Cellini 2 x vegetable soup 1 x steak + French fries 1 x lasagna 2 x mineral water	2 customers Name: Cellini 1 x vegetable soup 1 x lasagna 2 x steak + French fries 2 x mineral water	2 customers Name: Cellini 1 x vegetable soup 1 x lasagna 2 x steak + French fries 2 x mineral water 1 x ice cream

2 ▶ 7.3 Put the lines from the conversation in order. Then listen again and check.

 a Are you ready to order your main course? ____
 b Can I take your name? ____
 c The name's Cellini. ____
 d Of course. I'll just go and get it for you. ____
 e Would you like anything for dessert? ____
 f Could we just have the check, please? ____
 g Hello, do you have a table for eight o'clock this evening, please? ____
 h We have a table reserved in the name of Cellini. ____
 i For how many people? ____
 j It's for two people. ____
 k Hello, Giovanni's Restaurant. How can I help you? ____
 l Can I get you any drinks? ____
 m Ah yes, this way, please. ____
 n Would you like a starter? ____

3 ▶ 7.4 Complete the sentences for asking politely. Then listen and check.

 1 _____ both like the vegetable soup.
 2 I'd _____ the steak and French fries, please.
 3 _____ I have the lasagna, please?
 4 Can I _____ a glass of water, please?

4 Practice saying the sentences in exercise 3. Make sure you use polite intonation.

5 Reply to the waiter's questions. Use the information in parentheses.

 1 Hello, Moonlight Restaurant. How can I help? (you/table/three people?)
 2 Good evening, sir. Can I help you? (have/reserved/name/Smith)
 3 Would you like a starter? (like/chicken soup)
 4 Are you ready to order your main course? (can/have/large salad?)
 5 What would you like to drink? (could/have/apple juice?)
 6 Can I help you? (we/have/check?)

41

7 REVIEW and PRACTICE

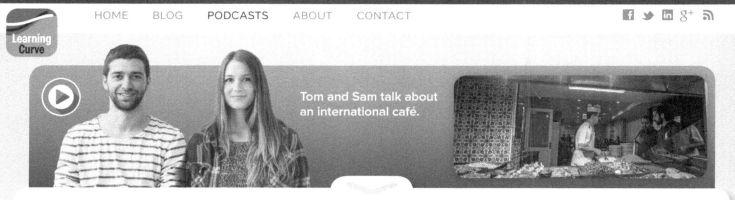

LISTENING

1 ▶ 7.5 Listen to the podcast about an international café. Number a–f in the order you hear them (1–6).

- a peppers ____
- b cheese ____
- c rice ____
- d tomatoes ____
- e cake ____
- f chicken ____

2 ▶ 7.5 Listen again. Are the sentences true (T) or false (F)?

1 Gabriela Romero is the manager of the international café. ____
2 People of different nationalities cook American food in the café. ____
3 The money from the café goes to charity. ____
4 Gabriela started the café alone. ____

3 ▶ 7.5 Listen again. Complete the sentences with one or two words.

1 Gabriela is from _____.
2 Gabriela lives in _____ now.
3 She made _____ burritos for her friends.
4 It costs $_____ to eat at the café.
5 Gabriela is making _____ for dinner.
6 The Turkish chef is making a big bowl of _____ pudding.

READING

1 Read the blog on page 43 about eating local food. Check (✓) the things Alex eats during the five days he describes.

- a mushrooms ____
- b orange juice ____
- c beans ____
- d carrots ____
- e cola ____
- f tomatoes ____
- g onions ____
- h cabbage ____
- i potatoes ____
- j eggs ____

2 Choose the correct answers.

1 Why doesn't he eat a lot of fruit?
  a They don't grow much fruit where he lives.
  b He doesn't really like it.
  c It's very expensive where he lives.
2 How does he feel at the start of the week?
  a He's excited – it's going to be fun.
  b He's not very excited – it won't be fun.
  c He's worried – he can't cook.
3 What does he eat on Day One?
  a nothing
  b porridge
  c supermarket cereal
4 Alex gets the ingredients for his omelet from
  a the supermarket.
  b the local store.
  c his aunt's backyard.
5 What happens when Alex goes to the local store?
  a He doesn't buy the things he planned to buy.
  b He pays too much money.
  c He forgets his shopping.
6 What doesn't Alex eat from his aunt's backyard on Day Five?
  a peppers
  b potatoes
  c cabbage

REVIEW and PRACTICE 7

HOME   BLOG   PODCASTS   ABOUT   CONTACT

Guest blogger Jack writes about eating local food.

Going local

Did you realize that the fruit and vegetables you eat can travel thousands of miles around the world before they reach you – and could be weeks old? That's why many people are trying to eat locally instead. I asked my friend, Alex McKay, from Scotland, to try to eat only local food for five days. Read his diary to find out what happened!

Day One

The weather here is often cold and rainy this time of year. We don't grow much fruit, so I'm not sure if this local only diet is going to be much fun!

For breakfast, I usually have a glass of orange juice and a bowl of supermarket cereal. Not today! I have some porridge from my grandmother (that's a kind of popular cereal in Scotland that's similar to oatmeal) and a cup of tea. The porridge tastes OK, and I find that I like knowing where my breakfast comes from.

Day Two

Today I go fishing in the river near my home. I'm really happy when (after a couple of hours) I catch a fish! I walk back and find a farmers' market selling potatoes and beans. These will make a perfect dinner with my delicious fresh fish!

Day Three

I'm not sure what to eat today. Luckily, my aunt comes to visit. She grows vegetables and she brings me some eggs, mushrooms, and onions. Great – I have the ingredients for an omelet. My aunt stays for dinner, and we eat together. This is much better than supermarket shopping!

Day Four

Today everything goes wrong! I go to the local store to buy some carrots for a healthy soup. But I come out with some cookies, a slice of cake, and two cans of cola. Not a healthy lunch!

Day Five

It's the last day! I cook some tasty stew with cabbage and peppers from my aunt's backyard, so I know they're fresh.

So how do I feel after my week of eating locally? Well, it can get a bit boring at times, but it's super healthy, and it's really good to know where your food comes from. Why not try it yourself?

UNIT 8 In the past

8A LANGUAGE

GRAMMAR: Past of *be*, *there was*, *there were*, and simple past: irregular verbs

1 Choose the correct options to complete the sentences.

1 ____ you good at sports when you were young?
 a Were b Was c Wasn't

2 We had a test yesterday. It ____ really difficult.
 a was b weren't c were

3 Last year, I visited Rome. It's very beautiful, but it ____ cheap!
 a was b were c wasn't

4 Why ____ you at the party last night?
 a was b wasn't c weren't

5 His parents ____ rich, but they had a big house.
 a was b were c weren't

6 It was a warm day, and there ____ lots of people in town.
 a was b were c wasn't

2 Complete the sentences with the simple past form of the verbs in parentheses.

Last week, I ¹____ (be) in New York. I ²____ (go) with my family: my mom, aunt, and two brothers. We ³____ (have) a really good time. Of course, we ⁴____ (see) all the sights – the Statue of Liberty, Central Park, and Times Square – and I ⁵____ (take) lots of photos. There are some great stores there, so I ⁶____ (buy) lots of new clothes – jeans, sneakers, and tops. We all loved the food, too – we ⁷____ (eat) some fantastic meals. We ⁸____ (come) home on Friday – but I want to go back again very soon!

VOCABULARY: Inventions

3 Complete the sentences with the words in the box.

digital camera toaster smartphone
microwave laptop dishwasher CD player

1 I couldn't live without my ____ in my pocket. I call my friends and play games on it, too!
2 We were late, but Mom left our dinner in the ____.
3 Our ____ is broken – the bread comes out black!
4 Suki's hobby is taking photos – she has a really expensive ____.
5 I don't enjoy washing the dishes after meals. I wish we had a ____.
6 Do your parents still listen to music on a ____?
7 I couldn't do my homework last night. My ____ broke, and I lost all my work!

4 Complete the conversation with the correct words.

Anna What kinds of things were there in your house when you were young, Grandma?

Grandma There wasn't a lot of technology in those days. For example, there was a radio, but we only had a black and white ¹____ to watch in the evenings, and we didn't have a DVD ²____.

Anna Really? And there was no ³____ TV?

Grandma Oh no, only black and white! And we didn't have a fridge or ⁴____ to keep our food cold, and there was no ⁵____ to dry your clothes when you washed them!

Anna But were you happy?

Grandma Yes, I was! Life was interesting. We didn't have a ⁶____ in our cars, so when you went somewhere new, you sometimes got lost. That was an adventure!

PRONUNCIATION: *was* and *were*

5 ▶ 8.1 Underline the words you think will be stressed. Then say the sentences. Listen, check, and repeat.

1 My grandmother's life was very interesting.
2 We weren't bored in school yesterday.
3 Her parents were both teachers.
4 There weren't many people in the market.
5 There was a bar of chocolate in the fridge.
6 I wasn't tired when I went to bed.
7 I told the waiter that my French fries were cold.
8 It wasn't very sunny last week.

44

SKILLS 8B

LISTENING: Listening for numbers, dates, and prices

1 Order the letters to make life stages.

1 EB RONB
_____

2 IFNSHI HLOOCS
_____

3 OG TO LGECLOE
_____

4 TEG REDIRMA
_____

5 EVAH A MAYFIL
_____

6 TGE VDECRODI
_____

7 TIREER
_____

2 ▶ 8.2 Listen to the description of a woman's life. Write the numbers of the four life stages in exercise 1 that you hear.

___ ___ ___ ___

3 ▶ 8.2 Listen again. Complete the sentences with numbers, dates, and prices.

1 Bertha wrote a book when she was _____ years old.
2 Bertha was born in _____.
3 Bertha and Fred had _____ children.
4 The camp was very popular in the _____s.
5 Bertha cooked meals for _____ people every day.
6 People stopped going to the camp in the _____s.
7 Fred died in _____.

4 Write the irregular past forms of the verbs from the audio.

1 begin _____
2 do _____
3 go _____
4 know _____
5 leave _____
6 take _____
7 think _____
8 meet _____

5 Order the words to make set phrases.

1 now / for / bye
_____!

2 of / would / cup / like / coffee / a / you
_____?

3 do / you / do / what
_____?

4 you / of / can / course
_____!

5 just / time / I'm / in
_____

6 a / tea / cup / of
_____.

7 of / paper / piece / a
_____.

8 all / of / first
_____

8C LANGUAGE

GRAMMAR: Simple past: regular verbs and past time expressions

1 Complete the time expressions with *last*, *ago*, *yesterday*, or *in*.

1 _____ week
2 two days _____
3 _____ 1975
4 _____ afternoon
5 a year _____
6 _____ evening
7 _____ the summer
8 three hours _____
9 _____ night
10 _____ the 21st century

2 Complete the sentences with the simple past form of regular verbs.

1 Where were you yesterday? I w_____ to see you.
2 It was a fantastic party! We d_____ all night.
3 We were friends when we were younger. We p_____ together every day.
4 "Did you have a good trip?" "Yes, I really e_____ it, thanks."
5 We p_____ a big party for Jen's birthday.
6 She s_____ really hard at school – that's why she has a good job now.
7 Sam t_____ to fix my bike, but it was no good – it was broken.
8 Diana o_____ the door and went inside, but no one was there.

3 Complete the conversations. Use the simple past form of the verbs in the box.

| want | use | not study | call | enjoy |
| fail | not save | watch | stop | not like |

1 "What did you do yesterday evening?" "Nothing much. We just _____ TV."
2 "How was your Spanish course?" "Terrible! I _____ so I _____ the exam!"
3 "What did you think of the new boss?" "I really _____ her."
4 "We _____ shopping online last month, but we _____ any money!"
5 "Were you busy last night? I _____ you but there was no answer." "I went swimming with my friend."
6 "How was the film yesterday?" "I really _____ it but Meg hated it!"
7 "Why did Emma leave?" "I think she _____ to get home early."
8 "This soup is horrible!" "Yes, I think I _____ too much salt."

4 Read the text and fill in blanks 1–8 with one word.

I ¹t_____ to Mexico to see my sister, Emma, ²l_____ summer. She met a Mexican man a few years ³_____ and moved to Mexico to marry him ⁴_____ 2015. I had a great time there! I ⁵s_____ in my sister's apartment in Mexico City, and we ⁶v_____ a lot of beautiful and interesting places together. She lives near a lot of good restaurants and cafés. We went out every night and I ⁷d_____ want to come home. ⁸Y_____ evening Emma called me. She wants me to go and visit her again next year!

PRONUNCIATION: -ed endings

5 ▶ 8.3 Circle the correct sound for the *-ed* endings. Listen, check, and repeat.

1 We tried to tell you, but you didn't listen.	/t/	/d/	/ɪd/
2 She decided to buy a new smartphone.	/t/	/d/	/ɪd/
3 They traveled across Africa by bicycle.	/t/	/d/	/ɪd/
4 Tom played with his toys in his bedroom.	/t/	/d/	/ɪd/
5 Katia liked reading books and listening to music.	/t/	/d/	/ɪd/
6 He waited all day to see her.	/t/	/d/	/ɪd/
7 Your mom looked very tired today.	/t/	/d/	/ɪd/
8 No one wanted to go to clubs.	/t/	/d/	/ɪd/
9 A police officer stopped the man's car.	/t/	/d/	/ɪd/
10 The bad weather ended in March.	/t/	/d/	/ɪd/

SKILLS 8D

WRITING: Planning and making notes

Last week, my friend Carla invited me on a date for the first time. At first, I was excited, but I didn't have a good day.

¹_____, I went to buy Carla some flowers.
²_____ I paid for them, I walked to the movie theater and waited outside. I waited there for almost an hour. When Carla arrived, she said, "Sorry – my phone's not working today!"
I was a bit annoyed, but I didn't say anything. ³_____, we went into the movie theater and watched a movie. Carla laughed a lot. I didn't know why, because it wasn't very funny.
⁴_____, in the evening, we went to a restaurant. Carla ordered an expensive meal, but I wasn't hungry. We talked about the movie and finished our food. ⁵_____, Carla looked in her bag and said, "Sorry – I don't have any money with me!"
We said goodbye ⁶_____ my bus arrived, but I was very tired and unhappy. I don't want to go on a date with Carla again!

1 Read the text about Roberto's day. Look at the pictures and write a–f in the correct order.

1 ____
2 ____
3 ____
4 ____
5 ____
6 ____

2 Read the text again. Fill in the blanks with the words in the box.

after   first   before   then (x2)   later

3 Answer the questions about Roberto's bad day.

1 When did it happen?
_____
2 How did Roberto feel at the start?
_____
3 What were the main events?
_____
4 How did Roberto feel after he said goodbye to Carla?
_____
5 What did Roberto think about Carla at the end?
_____

4 Write about a good or bad day you had. Use sequencers to show the order of events. Use the questions from exercise 3 to help you.

47

8 REVIEW and PRACTICE

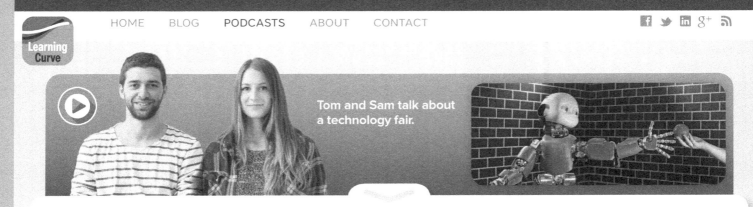

LISTENING

1 ▶ 8.4 Listen to the podcast about a technology fair. Which three inventions <u>don't</u> you hear?

a digital camera _____
b toaster _____
c smartphone _____
d freezer _____
e microwave _____
f (clothes) dryer _____

2 ▶ 8.4 Listen again. Choose the correct options to complete the sentences.

1 Izumi is *an inventor / a robot*.
2 Daichi is *an inventor / a robot*.
3 The robot can help *students / tourists*.

3 ▶ 8.4 Listen again. Complete the sentences with one or two words.

1 Tom was at the technology fair last _____.
2 Tom didn't buy a robot because it was very _____.
3 Daichi helps to guide people in big cities like _____.
4 The robot can show people how to _____ tickets for the subway.
5 Izumi studied technology _____.
6 It took Izumi _____ to make the robot.

READING

1 Read the blog on page 49 about a famous invention. Are the statements true (T) or false (F)?

1 Ruth Wakefield invented the chocolate chip cookie. _____
2 Ruth knew a lot about food and cooking. _____
3 The cookie's name comes from the name of a hotel. _____
4 She wrote a book about her life. _____
5 At first, Ruth didn't put any chocolate in the cookies. _____
6 When Ruth sold the recipe for the cookies, she made a lot of money. _____

2 Number sentences a–h in the correct order (1–8).

a Ruth got married. _____
b World War II began. _____
c A business bought Ruth's cookie recipe. _____
d Ruth opened a hotel. _____
e Ruth finished school. _____
f Ruth wrote a book about cooking. _____
g Ruth started her first job. _____
h Lots of people wrote to Ruth. _____

REVIEW and PRACTICE 8

HOME BLOG PODCASTS ABOUT CONTACT

Guest blogger Penny writes about an interesting story.

A tasty invention!

You may eat chocolate chip cookies every day, but you probably don't know anything about the woman who invented them! Here's the true story of Ruth Wakefield …

Ruth Wakefield was born in Massachusetts on June 17, 1903. She probably loved food from a young age because it was very important to her when she was older.

After she finished school, in 1924, she became a dietitian – someone who teaches people about food and how to have a healthy diet. In 1930, she bought a hotel called the Toll House Inn with her husband, Kenneth Donald Wakefield. It was very popular, and visitors came from all over the world. One of the most famous visitors was John F. Kennedy, before he became the president of the U.S. in 1961!

Ruth became famous for her excellent fish dinners and desserts, and in 1930, she wrote a very successful recipe book. Then, Ruth invented the chocolate chip cookie. It became really popular. Some people think that it was an accident and that Ruth wanted the chocolate to melt into the cookie. But the chocolate stayed solid, and that was the start of the cookie we all know and love today! The first recipe for how to make this famous cookie appeared in Ruth's cookbook in 1938.

During the Second World War, families sent chocolate chip cookies to their sons, brothers, and fathers who were soldiers a long way from home. They shared the cookies with other soldiers, and so lots of people tried them and loved them. Ruth started to get hundreds of letters from people who liked her cookies and who wanted more.

In the end, Ruth sold her recipe for Toll House Chocolate Crunch Cookies to a big company. Ruth only got one dollar for the recipe, but she also got a supply of chocolate for her whole life!

Ruth died in 1977 at the age of 73. Next time you bite into one of her delicious cookies, stop and think about the person who invented it!

UNIT 9 Education, education!

9A LANGUAGE

GRAMMAR: Simple past: questions

1 Choose the correct options to complete the questions.

1 What subjects *was / did / were* he study in college?
2 *What / Who / Why* was your favorite subject?
3 *What / When / Why* did you do after school?
4 *When / What / Who* was your best friend?
5 *Did / Was / Were* she have a lot of friends in kindergarten?
6 *Who / How / Where* did you eat lunch every day?
7 *Were / Was / Did* there a library in your elementary school?
8 *How / What / Where* did you play sports?
9 *Who / Where / How* was his first teacher in high school?
10 *Was / Did / Were* your teachers good?

2 Complete the conversation with past of *be* or simple past questions.

Sara ¹_____ were you yesterday? I called you three times.
Martin I was with Peter.
Sara Really? ²_____ did you do all day?
Martin First we went to the park, and later we played tennis.
Sara And ³_____ did you go after that?
Martin In the evening, we went to the movies.
Sara Ah, you went to the movies?
Martin Yes, I ⁴_____.
Sara ⁵_____ did you go with? Your friend Lisa?
Martin No, I ⁶_____. I told you, I went with Peter! What ⁷_____ you do all day?
Sara Well, I tried to call you. Then I called Peter.
Martin Ah! ⁸_____ he there?
Sara Yes, he ⁹_____. He was home. So, was he with you?
Martin Ah, no. He ¹⁰_____.

VOCABULARY: School subjects and education

3 Complete the text with the words in the box.

elementary   nursery   homework
college   exams   high school

In Scotland, children usually start ¹_____ school when they are three years old. They spend two years there, and then they go to ²_____ school when they are four or five. There they learn to read and write. They don't take ³_____ – they play a lot and learn by doing things. They start ⁴_____ when they are twelve. They work very hard, and have to do more ⁵_____ after school. If they do well, when they finish high school, students can go to ⁶_____ when they are about eighteen.

4 Complete the sentences.

1 I love learning about other countries so my favorite subject is g_____.
2 Ben hates m_____ because he isn't good with numbers.
3 Suki didn't study very hard so she f_____ her exam.
4 Which books are you reading in your L_____ class?
5 My little brother is only five, so he goes to k_____.
6 Victor decided to study L_____. He wants to speak French and Russian.
7 We love sports, so we always enjoy p_____ e_____ class.
8 When I finish school, I want to go to c_____.

PRONUNCIATION: Intonation in questions

5 ▶9.1 Read the questions. Do they have rising or falling intonation at the end? Listen, check, and repeat.

1 Did you go to kindergarten?
2 Why didn't you study art?
3 Who was your best friend in school?
4 Was the lesson interesting?
5 Did you have homework on the weekend?

SKILLS 9B

READING: Understanding words that you don't know

Meet three students who found out that it is never too late to learn!

Francisco Pardo

My dad was a self-employed builder. He had his own business and wanted me to go and work with him, ¹_____ I left high school at sixteen. I didn't like working as a builder, though – I was bored, ²_____ I started looking for something else. I bought a book about computer programming and read it from start to finish. Ten years later (and after a lot more reading and working with computers), I work for a computer company. I absolutely love it!

Bistra Nikolovo

I really liked school, but I thought that when I left college that was the end of learning. Then I discovered online studying. Last year I took courses on Shakespeare, in Italian, and on astronomy – I've always been interested in the stars! This year I'm doing Spanish and film making. I don't want to stop ³_____ I really enjoy learning this way!

Samantha Jones

I finished school without any real skills ⁴_____ I had my daughter when I was eighteen. When she started high school, I found that it was really tough helping her with her math homework. I had to do something about it, ⁵_____ I took a night class. My teacher was amazing, and I was really surprised that I could do the work. In the end, I went to college and studied teaching. I'm still doing that now – I work in an elementary school.

1 Read the text and answer each question with a word, a name or a number.

1 What did Francisco study after he left school?
  _____
2 What job did Francisco's father want him to do?
  _____
3 Who is taking online courses? _____
4 Which language did Bistra study last year?
  _____
5 How old was Samantha when she started a family?
  _____
6 What is Samantha's job? _____

2 Complete 1–5 in the text with *because* or *so*.

3 Find the words in the text. Are they nouns (N), adjectives (A), or verbs (V)?

1 bored _____
2 discovered _____
3 astronomy _____
4 skills _____
5 tough _____
6 amazing _____

4 Match 1–6 in exercise 3 with meanings a–f.

a something you learn from practice and study
b the study of the moon, stars, etc.
c not easy, difficult
d really good, surprising
e found out about
f not interested

51

9C LANGUAGE

GRAMMAR: Verb patterns: verb + *to* infinitive

1 Complete the text with *to* + the verbs in the box. There are two extra verbs.

> do   travel   move   make
> become   start   get   study

We're in our last year at school, and we're all planning what we want ¹_____ next year. Emile's family want ²_____ to Australia, so he's going to look for a job there. My friend Roberto hopes ³_____ a doctor after college. He needs ⁴_____ saving some money to pay for his studies. And me? I'm planning ⁵_____ English so I can teach it one day. I'd like ⁶_____ around the world with this job.

2 Complete the sentences with a *to* infinitive or the *-ing* form of the verbs in parentheses. Some sentences have two answers.

1. Do you like _____ in the sea? (swim)
2. We'd love _____ your new boyfriend! (meet)
3. Jack doesn't like _____ his parents' car. (drive)
4. William is learning _____ Japanese this year. (speak)
5. My uncle offered _____ us to the station. (take)
6. Would you like _____ in our new armchair? (sit)
7. They decided _____ married next year. (get)
8. Will he agree _____ you on Friday evening? (meet)
9. His dog loves _____ with a soccer ball in the park. (play)
10. Did Olivia choose _____ sneakers or sandals? (wear)

VOCABULARY: Resolutions

3 Choose the correct options to complete the text.

It's a new year and a new you! My name's Penelope Powers, and I'm a life coach. Do you want to get in shape and ¹____ more exercise? I can help you with your goals – and if you want to ²____ a marathon, I can make it happen! Perhaps you'd like more money. Do you want to ³____ a car or your dream house? Or maybe you need to ⁴____ a new job? I can give you lots of good ideas for when you ⁵____ an interview. Of course, relationships are important, too. When you work hard, it's difficult to ⁶____ someone new. I can help you ⁷____ a relationship or ⁸____ new friends. So, if you want to make a new start this year, let me know!

1. a be   b go   c get
2. a get   b run   c have
3. a buy   b make   c save
4. a be   b get   c earn
5. a have   b make   c save
6. a make   b meet   c join
7. a improve   b run   c meet
8. a be   b make   c lose

4 Complete the sentences with the correct verbs.

1. Tony really needs to _____ in shape. He drives everywhere and watches too much TV.
2. My boss isn't happy with me. She says I need to _____ more organized.
3. I love my job, but I'd like to _____ more money.
4. You don't need to _____ your diet. You already drink lots of water and eat healthy food.
5. We need to _____ some money if we want to go on vacation to Greece.
6. She wants to _____ weight. Her clothes are too small.
7. Oskar's planning to _____ a gym next month.
8. My sister's a salesclerk, but she wants to _____ a new job as a receptionist.

PRONUNCIATION: *'d like* and *like*

5 ▶9.2 Say the sentences. How do we say *'d like* and *like*? Listen, check, and repeat.

1. I'd like to go downtown this afternoon.
2. They'd like to have a barbecue.
3. We like eating healthy food.
4. I like my new boss.
5. We'd like to speak Spanish.
6. They like staying in shape.

SKILLS 9D

SPEAKING: Sounding sympathetic

1 ▶ 9.3 Listen to the conversation between two friends. Are the statements true (T) or false (F)?

1 Rakeem has a lot of English homework. ____
2 He did badly on an exam. ____
3 He wants to find a part-time job. ____
4 Rakeem needs some extra money. ____
5 He doesn't think it's a good idea to talk to his family. ____
6 He can't sleep because of his problems. ____
7 Talia thinks that the English teacher is a good person to ask for help. ____
8 Talia says that Rakeem needs to stay at home tonight. ____

2 ▶ 9.3 Order the words to make sentences from the conversation. Then listen again and check.

1 you / work / take / off / some / time / can / from
   _____?
2 should / not / I'm / sure / I
   _____.
3 don't / talk / with / why / you / your / family
   _____?
4 good / that's / a / idea
   _____.
5 visiting / tomorrow / about / your / how / teacher / English
   _____?
6 do / let's / fun / tonight / something
   _____!

3 ▶ 9.4 Talia talks to Rakeem about a problem that she's having. Complete the conversation. Then listen and check.

Rakeem	Is everything okay with you, Talia?
Talia	Yes, but my roommate is very noisy. It's difficult to study there.
Rakeem	Oh no! I'm sorry to hear that. ¹_____ you look for another apartment?
Talia	I'm not sure I ²_____. It's expensive to change apartments.
Rakeem	³_____ you talk to your roommate? Tell her that you need to study. I'm sure she'll try her best to be quieter.
Talia	That's a ⁴_____ idea.
Rakeem	How ⁵_____ studying when she's not at home?
Talia	Yes, maybe. She's not there this weekend! ⁶_____ have dinner at my apartment tomorrow night.
Rakeem	That's a ⁷_____ idea!

4 Complete the phrases for sounding sympathetic.

1 You _____ thing!
2 Oh no! I'm _____ to hear that!
3 That's a _____!
4 How _____!

5 ▶ 9.5 Listen to four situations. Respond using an expression from exercise 4. Sound sympathetic.

6 ▶ 9.6 Now listen to the situations again and write the response that you hear. Then listen again and repeat.

1 A I've fallen out with my sister. We're not speaking!
   B _____.
2 A I'm having a lot of problems with my boyfriend.
   B _____.
3 A That math exam was awful. I'm sure I failed it.
   B _____.
4 A I lost my wallet! And it had all my money in it.
   B _____.

9 REVIEW and PRACTICE

LISTENING

1 ▶9.7 Listen to the podcast about Belinda's school days. Check (✓) the subjects you hear.

a PE ___
b music ___
c math ___
d history ___
e IT ___
f languages ___
g literature ___
h art ___
i geography ___

2 ▶9.7 Listen again. Choose the correct options to answer the questions.

1 What kind of school did Belinda go to?
  a a school with no adults.
  b a school with no teachers.
2 Did Belinda like the school?
  a Yes, she was happy there.
  b No, she didn't like it.

3 ▶9.7 Listen again. Complete the sentences with one or two words.

1 Sam's favorite subjects were music _____.
2 Belinda finished school _____.
3 Now, she's studying art and _____ in college.
4 The adults at the school helped the students with any _____.
5 At the start of the week, the students worked in _____.
6 Belinda often went on trips to the _____ and _____.

READING

1 Read the blog on page 55 about someone who made a big change in his life. Number sentences a–e in the order the things happened (1–5).

a Aapo met lots of new people. ___
b Aapo's friends gave him advice about how to be happier. ___
c Aapo found out about an ice climbing club. ___
d Aapo decided not to go to college. ___
e Aapo felt very unhappy with his life. ___

2 Use the information in the blog to answer the questions with one or two words.

1 How old was Aapo when he decided to make a change in his life?
  _____
2 Where did his friends tell him to go to get exercise?
  _____
3 What did Aapo see that sounded interesting?
  _____
4 What did Aapo decide to learn more about?
  _____
5 Which other activity is like ice climbing?
  _____
6 Where does Aapo live?
  _____
7 What do you have to do so that you don't fall when you're climbing?
  _____
8 What is different about Aapo's life now?
  _____

REVIEW and PRACTICE 9

HOME   BLOG   PODCASTS   ABOUT   CONTACT

Guest blogger Taylor hears from a young man about how he changed his life.

LIFE CHANGES

Do you feel you need to make some resolutions? Perhaps you want to change your life, but you're not sure how to go about it? Here's Aapo Virtanen's story. He wanted to get in shape and lose weight, and thanks to a new hobby, everything changed.

It was a few months before my nineteenth birthday. I lived at home, didn't have a girlfriend, and I was overweight. School wasn't good either – I failed all my exams, and I didn't have the grades I needed to get into college. Nothing was going right!

My friends told me I needed to change. They said, "You should get more exercise and get in shape. And you really need to lose weight! Why not go to the gym?" But I don't like going to the gym – I just find it really boring. I wanted to do something different, but I wasn't sure what. Then I saw a poster about an ice climbing club. I didn't know what ice climbing was, but it sounded interesting, so I decided to find out more. I called the contact person and went to the first meeting. That was the beginning of a new life for me.

Ice climbing is an extreme sport. It's similar to rock climbing, but the rocks you climb are icy! I live in the north of Finland, so in the winter there is a lot of ice to climb. It's pretty dangerous, of course, but I love it. When you are ice climbing, you can't think about anything else. If you don't think carefully about what you are doing, you could fall. It makes your brain feel really alive, too. And I've made some great new friends doing it.

A year later, everything has changed – and everything's better! I'm in better shape, and I'm also very slim. I now realize that college isn't for me. I want to get a job so that I can earn money. I need to save a few hundred euros so that I can train to be an ice climbing teacher. Then I can ice climb all day, every day!

UNIT 10 People

10A LANGUAGE

GRAMMAR: Comparative adjectives

1 Complete the sentences with the comparative form of the adjectives in parentheses.

1 My grandparents' house is _____ than ours. (big)
2 Sam was _____ than his older brother. (friendly)
3 This exercise is _____ than the last one. (easy)
4 Which is _____ – New York or Paris? (far)
5 These boots are _____ than your old ones. (nice)
6 Is the weather _____ in the spring or the fall? (bad)
7 Walking in town is _____ than bike riding. (safe)
8 The food in this café is _____ than my cooking! (good)
9 It was _____ yesterday than it is today. (hot)
10 The bus was _____ than the train. (fast)

2 Use the prompts to write sentences.

1 most stores / bit / expensive / the market
   _____
2 New York / much / crowded / my city
   _____
3 the library / quiet / our classroom
   _____
4 skiing / lot / dangerous / walking
   _____!
5 the park / noisy / a club
   _____
6 your niece / smart / your nephew
   _____?

VOCABULARY: Adjectives to describe places

3 Choose the correct options to complete the sentences.

1 We need to go shopping. The fridge and cabinets are _____!
   a safe   b crowded   c empty
2 I can't see anything at all outside. It's really _____.
   a ugly   b dark   c light
3 It can be _____ with so many fast cars on the road.
   a unfriendly   b great   c dangerous
4 Sasha didn't like her new school. Everyone was very _____.
   a beautiful   b unfriendly   c crowded
5 I made some vegetable soup yesterday, but it tasted _____!
   a horrible   b ugly   c dark
6 It was a _____ day, so they decided to go to the beach.
   a friendly   b beautiful   c safe

4 Complete the sentences with adjectives with the opposite meaning.

1 Everyone loves Anna. She's a really *unfriendly* _____ girl.
2 Is it *dangerous* _____ to go out at night in your city?
3 Look at that building! Don't you think it's *beautiful* _____?
4 The streets in this town aren't very *dark* _____ at night.
5 I don't like taking the bus because it's always *empty* _____.
6 This pizza is really *terrible* _____. Would you like some?

PRONUNCIATION: -er endings

5 ▶10.1 Say the sentences. How do we say the comparative adjectives? Listen, check, and repeat.

1 Her shoes were cheaper than mine.
2 The country is quieter than the city.
3 You're always busier than me!
4 Is your car safer than Alex's?
5 Anna was friendlier than her cousin.
6 Is Madrid bigger than Barcelona?
7 His hair was darker than yours.
8 It's noisier here than in class.

SKILLS 10B

LISTENING: Listening for detailed information (1)

1 ▶10.2 You will hear an interview about a model agency. Check (✓) the words you think you'll hear. Then listen and check.

a elderly   ____
b slim   ____
c tall   ____
d thin   ____
e bald   ____
f young   ____
g overweight ____
h middle-aged ____

2 ▶10.2 Listen again. Write the words you hear instead of the underlined words.

1 He owns a model agency. ____
2 Their appearance is very different. ____
3 Many of us are bored with seeing beautiful models. ____
4 I really liked clothes and fashion. ____
5 Models don't always need to be pretty. ____
6 At first, it wasn't easy. ____

3 ▶10.2 Read the questions carefully. Then listen again and choose the correct answers.

1 When did Leon start his model agency business?
   a last year
   b five months ago
   c three years ago
2 What does Leon say about his models?
   a They don't look like most models.
   b They are all very beautiful.
   c They are all young.
3 Why didn't Leon become a model?
   a He didn't want to change his appearance.
   b He didn't like his hair.
   c He wanted a more traditional job.
4 What does Leon say is important for a model?
   a lots of clothes
   b a good appearance
   c his or her character
5 How successful is Leon's business?
   a It's not very successful at all.
   b It's doing better now.
   c It's changing all the time.

4 Order the letters to make appearance words.

1 D L N O B   ____
2 U C Y L R   ____
3 G R R E I N A   ____
4 S T H C M U E A   ____
5 A F I R   ____
6 M M D U I E - H E L N T G   ____
7 Y G R A   ____
8 A B E D R D E   ____
9 N P G I I R C E   ____
10 S S S G L A E   ____

5 ▶10.3 Read the sentences and underline the words that you think have weak forms. Listen and check.

1 I mean, their appearance is pretty different!
2 My models are very different from usual models.
3 What an interesting idea!
4 At first, it was difficult.
5 People like looking at my models.

57

10C LANGUAGE

GRAMMAR: Superlative adjectives

1 Complete the sentences with the superlative forms of the adjectives in the box.

> good bad big safe
> crowded old far friendly

1 This magazine says that _____ person in the country is 112!
2 Which is _____ star from Earth?
3 Alberto won a competition for _____ painting in the art class.
4 That's _____ cake in the store! We only need a small one.
5 What's _____ city in Europe? I want to go traveling on my own.
6 I got _____ score on the test – I didn't get any answers right!
7 Mumbai is _____ city in India. About twenty million people live there.
8 Who is _____ teacher in your school?

2 Complete the text with the correct words.

I go to a photography club every Thursday, and last week we gave out end-of-year prizes. Everybody likes Sara, so we decided she was the ¹_____ popular girl in the club. Ben is friends with everyone – so he got a prize for ²_____ nicest person. Lucy always takes fantastic pictures – she got a prize for the ³_____ photo. But Mara took the ⁴_____ exciting photo – it was of a car race. Her dad had the ⁵_____ car, so he won. It was a great evening, and I was really happy. In fact, I think it was one of the ⁶_____ days of my life!

VOCABULARY: Personality adjectives

3 Order the letters to make personality adjectives.

1 He is very **neitcdonf** in France because he speaks French well.
_____
2 She's really **onersgue**. She always gets me a birthday present.
_____
3 It is important to be **tolepi** by opening doors for people.
_____
4 I like **relfhuec** people who smile a lot.
_____
5 She is not very **kavtlieta**. I think she is shy.
_____
6 My sister is really **sratm**. She passed all her exams.
_____

4 Complete the personality adjectives.

1 Max can't swim, so he was very b_____ to jump into the water.
2 We all laugh a lot when Wahid's here. He's a really f_____ student.
3 "Can I carry your bag for you?" "Thanks, that's extremely k_____."
4 Our cat's very l_____. It sleeps most of the day.
5 My sister's not s_____ at all – she makes friends with everyone.
6 Everyone likes my chemistry teacher, but my music teacher's not very p_____.

PRONUNCIATION: Superlative adjectives

5 ▶ 10.4 Say the sentences. How do we say the superlative adjectives? Listen, check, and repeat.

1 What's the most exciting place in the world?
2 She's the kindest girl I know.
3 He is the laziest boy in the school.
4 Ella is the most popular girl in the club.
5 It's the funniest movie of the year.
6 Who's the most relaxed person in your family?
7 Is she the most beautiful woman in the country?
8 My nicest present was this necklace.

SKILLS 10D

WRITING: Writing a description of a person

A WOMAN I ADMIRE

A Florence Nightingale was born in 1820 in Florence, Italy, but her family was British. After a year, they moved back to England. Later, Florence became a nurse and helped a lot of people. She was an attractive, slim woman with long brown hair and a lovely smile.

B Florence's parents wanted her to get married, but she decided to travel and to learn about the science of nursing. She was a nurse in hospitals in Turkey during the Crimean war against Russia. These hospitals were dangerous and very dirty, and it was extremely difficult working there. Florence tried very hard to make the hospitals cleaner and safer places.

C I admire Florence Nightingale because she was strong and one of the bravest women at that time. Women usually stayed at home then, but Florence did what she thought was right. Her story inspired me, and I want to be a nurse, too.

1 Read the text about Florence Nightingale. Which paragraphs give the information below? Write A, B, or C.

1 why the writer admires her ____
2 facts about her life ____
3 where she was from ____
4 what she believed ____
5 what her job was ____
6 what she looked like ____

2 Complete the sentences about Florence Nightingale. Use a verb from the box in the simple past.

| travel | make | do | work | not be |
| be (x2) | not want | help | want | become |

1 Florence Nightingale _____ Italian, but she _____ born in Italy.
2 She _____ to get married. She _____ a nurse, instead.
3 She _____ to learn about nursing, so she _____ to Turkey.
4 She _____ in hospitals in Turkey and tried to make them safer.
5 She _____ a lot of soldiers and _____ what she thought was right.
6 She _____ a brave and attractive woman, and _____ a real difference to people's lives.

3 Join the sentences using a clause with *when*. Write two versions for each sentence.

Example

When she was young, she lived in Italy. / She lived in Italy when she was young.

1 Florence was a baby. That's when her family moved to England.
   _____
   _____

2 There was a war against Russia. At that time, Florence worked as a nurse.
   _____
   _____

3 Florence was young. At that time, women usually stayed at home.
   _____
   _____

4 Write a description of someone you admire. Include the information below:

Paragraph 1: Where is he/she from? What does he/she do? What does he/she look like?

Paragraph 2: What are the important events and achievements in his/her life?

Paragraph 3: Why do you admire this person?

10 REVIEW and PRACTICE

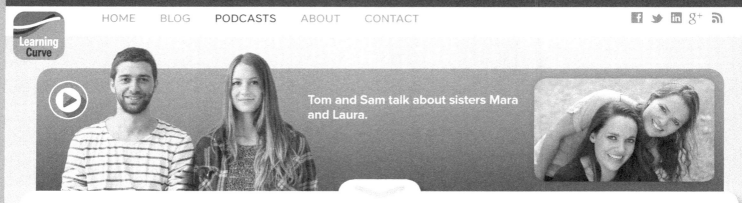

LISTENING

1 ▶ 10.5 Listen to the podcast about two sisters. Choose the correct answers.

1 What do Mara and Laura do?
   a Mara's a theater director and Laura's an actress.
   b They're both actresses.
2 Do they have similar personalities and appearance?
   a Yes, they do.
   b No, they don't.

2 ▶ 10.5 Listen again. Are the sentences about Mara (M) or Laura (L)?

1 She was a quiet and polite child. ____
2 She's two years older than her sister. ____
3 She's tall and slim. ____
4 She has long, black hair. ____
5 She's a little overweight. ____
6 She has brown, curly hair. ____

3 ▶ 10.5 Listen again. Are the sentences true (T) or false (F)?

1 Mara works at a theater in Madrid. ____
2 Laura is less famous than her sister. ____
3 Mara often has a lot of problems with Laura. ____
4 Mara often plays talkative or funny characters. ____
5 Mara prefers the parts that her sister plays. ____

READING

1 Read the blog on page 61 about some of the best places in the world to visit. What does the blog say? Choose the correct options to complete the sentences.

1 The best view is from the *Grand Canyon* / *Mount Ararat*.
2 Reykjavik is one of the *coldest* / *friendliest* cities.
3 The people in Auckland are very *kind* / *shy*.
4 Switzerland is the *most dangerous* / *safest* country.
5 Scottish people are the *nicest* / *most talkative*.

2 Complete the sentences with one or two words from the blog.

1 Mount Ararat is a very tall _____ in Turkey.
2 Readers decided that the _____ city in the world is Auckland.
3 One reader said that he/she talked to lots of _____ when he/she was in New Zealand.
4 The places that are safe to visit aren't always _____, as well.
5 A female traveler said she was happy walking in _____ of Switzerland at night.
6 Readers said that the Czech Republic, Denmark, and Canada were also very _____ places.
7 The _____ food was the deep-fried bar of chocolate.

REVIEW and PRACTICE 10

HOME   BLOG   PODCASTS   ABOUT   CONTACT

Tom and Sam look at the best and worst places to visit.

▶ You have your say

We all love traveling, but what are the best – and the worst – places to go to? Here are some of our readers' ideas. Do you agree with them?

BEST VIEW

Many people think that the best view is the Grand Canyon in Arizona, but 60% of our readers say that Mount Ararat in Turkey is even more beautiful! This 5,000-meter-high volcano is an awesome sight – if you go there, take a picnic and make sure you have your camera with you!

FRIENDLIEST CITY

We often think of cities as crowded places where people never stop to speak to each other. It doesn't have to be this way! Many of you voted for Reykjavik in Iceland. The weather may be cold, but the people are not unfriendly – lots of our readers wrote in to say how kind and welcoming people in this city are. However, in our readers' opinion, the people of Auckland, New Zealand are even happier to talk. One traveler said, "I can't count the number of times strangers came up and started speaking to me. And on a three-week visit I got invited to dinner five times. Wow!"

SAFEST COUNTRY FOR VISITORS

Sadly, some of the most exciting countries in the world can also be quite dangerous. But safe doesn't have to mean boring. Our readers voted the lovely mountainous Switzerland as the safest country to visit. One female traveler said, "I feel totally safe walking around at night, even when it's dark, and the streets are empty." Sounds good to us! Denmark, Canada, and the Czech Republic were also on the top of the safe places list.

WORST DISH

We're sorry, Scotland, but the prize goes to you! Many people voted for a deep-fried chocolate bar. One reader said, "This was horrible. I need to lose weight! I didn't want to eat a deep-fried dessert." We hope our Scottish readers don't feel too bad though – our readers also think Scotland has the nicest people!

UNIT 11

On the move

11A LANGUAGE

GRAMMAR: *Have to/don't have to*

1 Choose the correct options to complete the sentences.

1 She ___ save money because she's going to college next year.
   a have to   b don't have to   c has to

2 Do you ___ take the train or can you ride your bike?
   a have to   b have   c has to

3 He ___ go to work this morning.
   a have to   b doesn't have to
   c don't have to

4 You ___ wash the dishes – I can do it.
   a don't have to   b have to   c has to

5 We ___ visit our grandfather tomorrow.
   a has to   b doesn't have to   c have to

6 I ___ have to go to bed early because it's Saturday!
   a has   b don't   c doesn't

7 She ___ do her homework before she can play online games.
   a has to   b have to   c don't have to

8 Are you coming to New Zealand? You ___ visit me!
   a doesn't have to   b has to   c have to

2 Complete the e-mail with the correct form of *have to/don't have to*.

Dear Maria,

How are you? Dad and I are both well. Ella is working in a store on Saturdays because she ¹_____ to save money to buy clothes! What is your house like? Is it near your college? Do you ²_____ to take the bus, or can you walk? I hope you ³_____ have to get up too early in the morning! Are you eating well? Remember, it ⁴_____ have to be expensive to cook a delicious meal. I hope you can come home next weekend for your brother's birthday. So you don't ⁵_____ to do your wash this week, I can do it when you're here. What are you doing tomorrow? I ⁶_____ have to get up early because it's Sunday. And your father? Yes, he ⁷_____ because he ⁸_____walk the dog!

Love from Mom X

VOCABULARY: Travel and transportation

3 Order the letters to make words for travel and transportation.

1 The New York *yuwsba* _____ is often very crowded.
2 When my grandmother was 80, she had a ride in a *poctrelieh* _____.
3 You have to wear a helmet to travel by *toromylcec* _____.
4 Lots of people travel by *restoco* _____ in Italy.
5 Our *rryef* _____ takes five hours to cross the sea.
6 I prefer to travel by *sbu* _____. It's cheap and relaxing.

4 Look at the pictures. Write the words.

1 _____   3 _____   5 _____
2 _____   4 _____   6 _____

PRONUNCIATION: *have to/has to*

5 ▶11.1 Say the sentences. How do we say *have to* and *has to*? Listen, check, and repeat.

1 Does she have to speak English at work?
2 Do you have to go to bed early?
3 He doesn't have to cook this evening.
4 He has to finish his homework.
5 You have to visit me in Turkey.
6 I don't have to work tomorrow.

62

SKILLS 11B

READING: Reading for detail

Two friends, two different opinions ...

Best friends Cara and Vanessa went on vacation together for the first time this summer. Are they still friends? Read and find out!

Vanessa

I was so happy when Cara and I decided to go on vacation together this summer. Cara is my best friend, and I was really looking forward to it. In the end, though, it wasn't so great.

Cara is very energetic, but I like to relax on vacation. She wanted to take the train and go sightseeing in different towns and cities – but I wanted to stay on the beach! She said, "You're on vacation! You have to see things! You can't just sleep all the time."

We spent a lot of money on sightseeing and other activities. I don't think you have to spend money to have fun. Maybe Cara disagrees with that, though!

We will definitely stay friends, but we probably won't go on vacation together again.

Cara

Vanessa is a really great friend, and we had a wonderful vacation together. She was a bit tired sometimes – maybe that was just because the weather was too hot.

We did so many fun things – we took a ferry to a little island, we walked for miles through beautiful countryside, and I think we saw all the sights, too. One day we even did a parachute jump! That was certainly my favorite part of the trip.

Next summer, we're probably going on vacation together again. Possibly a sports vacation next time? I can't wait!

1 Look at the title and the pictures. What do you think the text is about?

　a　two friends who had a great vacation together
　b　two friends who don't feel the same about their vacation
　c　two friends who had a terrible vacation together

2 Read the questions and options. Fill in the blanks with the words in the box. There are two extra words.

　do　Cara　best　time　Vanessa　feel　money

　1　How did Vanessa _____ before she went on vacation with Cara?
　　a　happy and excited
　　b　tired and sad
　　c　bored
　2　What did Vanessa want to _____ on vacation?
　　a　go sightseeing
　　b　relax on the beach
　　c　travel by train
　3　Why did they spend a lot of _____?
　　a　Their hotel was expensive.
　　b　They ate in expensive restaurants.
　　c　They did a lot of sightseeing.
　4　What did Cara like _____ about the trip?
　　a　the parachute jump
　　b　the weather
　　c　the ferry trip
　5　What type of vacation does _____ want them to go on next year?
　　a　a beach vacation
　　b　a sports vacation
　　c　a shopping vacation

3 Now choose the correct options to answer the questions in exercise 2.

4 Order the words to make sentences.

　1　go on vacation / I / with Vanessa / want to / next year /definitely
　　_____
　2　prefers / vacations / maybe / relaxing / Vanessa
　　_____
　3　spent / we / too / money / much / probably
　　_____
　4　going on / sports vacation / a / next summer / possibly / we're
　　_____
　5　enjoyed / her / my vacation / I / with / certainly
　　_____
　6　our friend / is going / to come / next year / Mandy / perhaps
　　_____

63

11C LANGUAGE

GRAMMAR: *Be going to* and future time expressions

1 Choose the correct options to complete the sentences.

1 *Are / Is / Am* your girlfriend going to come with us?
2 I *'m not / 're not / 's not* going to finish all these French fries.
3 "Are you going to eat that slice of bread?" "Yes, I *is / are / am*."
4 They *'s not going / not going / 're not going* to stay at a hotel.
5 "Is he going to be late for class again?" "No, he *'s not / 're not / is*."
6 *Are / Is / Am* you going to buy some new clothes?
7 We *isn't going / are going / not going* to visit Paris this month.
8 "Are the children going to get dressed soon?" "Yes, they *aren't / is / are*."

2 Complete the text with the correct form of *going to*.

I'm really excited about my plans for the summer. First, I ¹_____ work for two weeks in a café. I ²_____ go out because I have to save money. After that, my cousin Kinga ³_____ come to visit me from Hungary. We ⁴_____ go traveling around Europe. I can't wait! Her parents ⁵_____ come to my house, too, but they ⁶_____ go traveling with us. Kinga and I ⁷_____ take the bus – the train is much faster. Where ⁸_____ stay? I don't know yet! But I know it ⁹_____ be anywhere expensive, because Kinga ¹⁰_____ have much money.

VOCABULARY: Vacation activities

3 Choose the correct options to complete the e-mail.

Hi Carla,

I'm having a great time here in Crete! It's a really beautiful place. We're ¹____ at a hotel near the sea. You know I love relaxing on the ²____ or ³____ the pool, so this is perfect for me! We're here for ten days before we come home.

There's only one problem. Mom and Dad want us to ⁴____ sightseeing and visit ⁵____. I don't want to! It's really hot, and I don't enjoy looking at old buildings!

My brother Sam is having a lot of fun, too. He ⁶____ surfing all day, every day!

See you soon,
Daphne

	a	b	c
1	staying	going	visiting
2	mountains	beach	surfing
3	by	on	to
4	be	get	go
5	campsites	museums	mountains
6	has	does	goes

4 Complete the sentences.

1 We went on v_____ to Florida. It rained every day!
2 I really want to go swimming. Can we go to the b_____ later?
3 In the summer, I love sitting by the p_____ reading a book.
4 We enjoy walking, so we're going h_____ in Peru.
5 Where did you stay? Were you at a c_____?
6 Mario loves old paintings – he wants to v_____ an art gallery tomorrow.

PRONUNCIATION: Sentence stress

5 ▶ 11.2 Say the sentences. Listen and repeat.

1 I'm going to stay with friends.
2 We're going to be more organized.
3 You're not going to run a marathon.
4 He's not going to have an interview.
5 Is she going to swim with us?
6 Are you going to see Ernesto tonight?

SKILLS 11D

SPEAKING: Checking information

1 ▶ 11.3 Listen to the conversation at a hotel. Choose the correct answers.

1 Mr Gutiérrez is staying at the Amberton Hotel for ___ nights.
   a three   b four   c five

2 He is staying on the ___ floor.
   a seventh   b eighth   c ninth

3 They start breakfast at ___ in the morning.
   a seven   b eight   c nine

2 ▶ 11.3 Complete the conversation with the words in the box. Listen again and check.

| spell | checking | password | sign | reservation |
| floor | reserved | key | breakfast | ID |

Receptionist Good afternoon. Welcome to the Amberton Hotel. ¹_____ in?
Mr Gutiérrez Yes. I have a ²_____ under the name of Gutiérrez.
Receptionist Could you ³_____ your last name, please?
Mr Gutiérrez Yes, it's G-U-T-I-E-R-R-E-Z.
Receptionist You've ⁴_____ for three nights and are checking out on Friday. Is that correct?
Mr Gutiérrez Yes, that's right.
Receptionist Ah, yes. Can I have your ⁵_____, please?
Mr Gutiérrez Yes, of course.
Receptionist Can you ⁶_____ this form, please? OK. Here's your ⁷_____. You're on the ninth floor.
Mr Gutiérrez What's the WiFi ⁸_____?
Receptionist It's Amberton, the name of the hotel.
Mr Gutiérrez Great, thanks! And what time is ⁹_____?
Receptionist It's from seven to nine.
Mr Gutiérrez Thank you. Which ¹⁰_____ did you say? The eighth?
Receptionist The ninth. Enjoy your stay.
Mr Gutiérrez Thank you!

3 Complete the phrases to check information.

1 You've reserved for six nights and are checking out on Friday. Is that _____?
2 Thank you. My room's on the seventh floor, _____?
3 _____ you say breakfast starts at eight thirty?

4 Are the phrases in exercise 3 formal (F), neutral (N), or informal (I)?

1 _____
2 _____
3 _____

5 ▶ 11.4 Listen to five sentences. Who says them? Write receptionist (R) or guest (G).

1 _____
2 _____
3 _____
4 _____
5 _____

6 ▶ 11.4 Listen again. Respond and check the information with the receptionist or guest.

7 You are a guest in a hotel. Respond to the receptionist's comments. Use a formal (F), neutral (N), or informal (I) phrase.

1 **Receptionist** "Dinner is from 7:30 p.m. to 9:45 p.m."
   You _____ (N)

2 **Receptionist** "The price for a double room is $125."
   You _____ (F)

3 **Receptionist** "There's WiFi in every room."
   You _____ (I)

4 **Receptionist** "Your room is on the eleventh floor."
   You _____ (N)

5 **Receptionist** "There's a gym in the hotel."
   You _____ (F)

6 **Receptionist** "Breakfast's not included in the price."
   You _____ (N)

11 REVIEW and PRACTICE

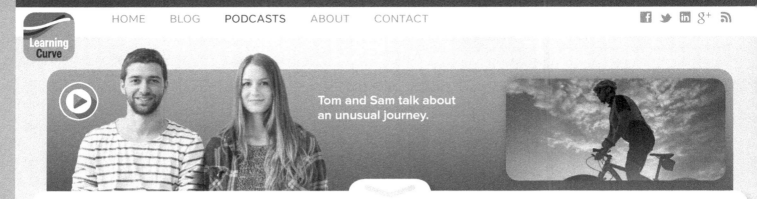

LISTENING

1 ▶ 11.5 Listen to the podcast about an unusual trip. Are the sentences about Ben true (T) or false (F)?

1 He finished his trip in the spring. ____
2 He is traveling to places that begin with the same letter. ____
3 He is planning to visit the beach. ____
4 He will go sightseeing in Bolivia. ____
5 He is going to Tokyo next year. ____

2 ▶ 11.5 Listen again. Choose the correct answers.

1 Where did Ben start his trip after his flight?
   a Belgium
   b Britain
   c Budapest
2 How is Ben going to travel to Bolivia?
   a by plane
   b by bike
   c by bus
3 Ben's not working for ____ months.
   a three
   b four
   c six
4 What does Ben say is interesting about Bosnia?
   a its beaches
   b the history
   c everything
5 Where will Ben go surfing?
   a Bosnia
   b Belize
   c Bolivia
6 Which of the places doesn't Ben mention?
   a Toledo
   b Tokyo
   c Turkey

READING

1 Read the blog on page 67 about vacation jobs. Complete the sentences with *Kyra*, *Oliver*, or *Stefano*.

1 _____ had a job working with older people.
2 _____ is going to teach children art.
3 _____ stayed at a campsite last year.
4 _____ went to the Mediterranean.
5 _____ worked in two different countries.
6 _____ likes working with children.

2 Are the sentences true (T), false (F), or doesn't say (DS)?

1 You need a lot of money to travel around the world. ____
2 You have to be in shape to pick fruit. ____
3 Picking fruit is an easy job and it pays well. ____
4 Kyra ate a lot of fruit when she was in France. ____
5 You can do different kinds of jobs on a cruise ship. ____
6 Oliver didn't like working on a cruise ship. ____
7 The people working on a cruise ship have to be young. ____
8 You have to like children to work at some campsites. ____
9 Stefano is going to teach the children English. ____
10 At the vacation camp, the children can go hiking. ____

REVIEW and PRACTICE 11

HOME   BLOG   PODCASTS   ABOUT   CONTACT

Guest blogger Penny writes about working in different countries.

Work your way around the world

Do you want to go traveling, but you have no money? Don't worry! You don't have to be rich to see the world. There are lots of ways you can visit different countries and earn money at the same time. Here are some of my top ideas.

FRESH AIR AND FRUIT

This is a popular way for young people to travel the world. You can pick grapes in France, oranges in Spain, and olives in Greece. You have to be in shape and enjoy outdoor life, but it's a lot of fun, and you can make friends from lots of different countries. Kyra Scott traveled around Europe picking fruit last year: "I started in the UK, where I picked strawberries. Then I went to France and picked peaches. It can be hard work, and I didn't earn much money. But I made enough to pay for the campsite and to buy food. I also had as much fruit as I could eat – I don't think I ever want to see another strawberry!"

SAIL AWAY

Cruise ships take thousands of vacationers every year to some of the world's most beautiful towns and cities, so they're always looking for staff to wash dishes, serve food, or clean the cabins. You have to work long hours, but the pay can be pretty good. Oliver Baum worked on a cruise ship this summer, traveling around the Mediterranean: "It was a fantastic experience. The guests were all elderly, and they were mostly really polite and friendly. I really enjoyed looking after them!"

WORK AT A VACATION CAMP

If you like working with other people, why not look for a job at a campsite? Vacation camps are always looking for young people to help with entertainment and activities. If you like children, this can be an excellent job. Stefano Rossi says: "I'm going to work at a campsite in Spain next year. I'm going to look after children in the morning. They do painting and drama and lots of other activities, like surfing. You don't have to speak Spanish, as lots of the vacationers are American or British – but it helps if you do!"

You see? No money – no problem! Start making your travel plans now!

UNIT 12 Enjoy yourself

12A LANGUAGE

GRAMMAR: Present perfect with *ever* and *never*

1 Order the words to make sentences and questions in the present perfect.

1 ever / you / the Northern Lights / seen / have
_____?

2 have / a blog / written / they / never
_____.

3 has / this book / read / he / ever
_____?

4 gone / never / together / we've / bowling
_____.

5 ever / we / your sister-in-law / have / met
_____?

6 has / never / karate / done / he
_____.

2 Complete the conversation with the present perfect form of the verbs in parentheses.

Marta I'm having a party on Saturday! Do you want to help? I need to be really organized!

Piotr [1]_____ (I/never/organize) a party before. But I'd love to help!

Marta Great, thanks. [2]_____ (you/ever/make) pizza?

Piotr No, [3]_____ (I/not)!

Marta That's OK. [4]_____ (I/never/make) one either!

Piotr [5]_____ (Sam/ever/cook) for a party? We could ask him.

Marta Great idea! [6]_____ (he/have) lots of parties. [7]_____ (I/be) to some of them.

Piotr But [8]_____ (I/not/see) him this week. Is he at home?

Marta Oh no! I remember now. [9]_____ (he/leave) to visit his aunt and uncle in Germany! He comes back next week.

VOCABULARY: Entertainment

3 Complete the text with the words in the box. There is one extra word.

concerts   artist   singer   match   exhibit   bands   opera

Although my town is small, there's a lot to do. This weekend, I went to a really interesting art [1]_____ at the gallery near my house. I saw some beautiful paintings. I met the [2]_____ and it was really interesting hearing him talk about his work. My city is also famous for music. There's a festival every year, and many [3]_____ from different countries come to play. There's a small jazz club near my house, too. It stays open late and has great [4]_____! If you prefer classical music, you can see an [5]_____. I love the music – when I was younger I wanted to be an opera [6]_____. It didn't happen, but I still love watching and dreaming!

4 Complete the words.

1 We love movies with Daniel Radcliffe. He's a brilliant a_____r.

2 The basketball p_____s were really happy when their team won.

3 I saw *Swan Lake* at the theater last night. It's my favorite b_____t.

4 How many m_____s are in the band?

5 I don't mind watching baseball on TV, but I've never been to a g_____e.

6 There were two d_____s and a traditional Spanish guitarist in the show.

PRONUNCIATION: Sentence stress

5 ▶12.1 Say the sentences. Listen and repeat.

1 Have you ever been to this gallery?
2 I've never played the violin.
3 I've served food in a café.
4 Have you ever been to a rock concert?
5 I haven't tried Vietnamese food.
6 I haven't been to Canada.
7 I've been to Poland.
8 I've never written a song.

SKILLS 12B

LISTENING: Listening for detailed information (2)

1 ▶12.2 Listen to the conversation about birthdays. Which adjectives describe the things below?

1 Layla's last birthday — amazing / boring / terrible
2 Peter's last birthday — stupid / awesome / strange
3 the ending of the movie — sad / interesting / exciting
4 the Thanksgiving costumes — awful / scary / fun

2 ▶12.2 Listen again. Choose the correct answers.

1 Who is Ben?
  a Layla's father
  b Layla's friend
  c Layla's cousin
2 How did Layla get to Vancouver?
  a by bus
  b by train
  c by car
3 Who took Peter to see a play?
  a his girlfriend
  b Layla
  c his best friend
4 When is Layla's birthday?
  a November 22nd
  b November 23rd
  c November 24th
5 What kind of party does Peter suggest?
  a a surprise party
  b a costume party
  c a strange party

3 Listen again. Answer the questions. Write complete sentences.

1 How many of Layla's friends and family were on the train to Vancouver?

2 How long did Layla and her friends and family go to Vancouver for?

3 How did Peter's girlfriend feel after the movie?

4 Has Layla had a costume party before?

4 ▶12.3 Read the sentences. Mark the links between words. Listen, check, and repeat.

1 Last year I had an amazing birthday.
2 My cousin organized a surprise party for me.
3 I thought I was going to see an action movie.
4 Everyone can get dressed up in really fun costumes.
5 I had one when I was eight years old.

69

12C LANGUAGE

GRAMMAR: Present perfect and simple past

1 Choose the correct options to complete the sentences.

1 We _____ Cara last night. She looked great.
   a have seen
   b saw
2 _____ a letter to a famous person as a child?
   a Have you ever written
   b Did you ever write
3 Last week they _____ the new pizza restaurant.
   a tried
   b have tried
4 I _____ any of the *Harry Potter* movies.
   a have never seen
   b never saw
5 When _____ to the gym this morning?
   a have you been
   b did you go
6 She _____ her boyfriend in school.
   a met
   b has met
7 Where _____ that new watch?
   a have you bought
   b did you buy
8 "Has she ever been to Mexico?" "No, she _____."
   a didn't
   b hasn't
9 How _____ on their exams last month?
   a did they do
   b have they done
10 "Have your grandparents ever used a smartphone?" "No, they _____."
   a haven't
   b didn't
11 Who _____ at the party yesterday?
   a have you spoken to
   b did you speak to
12 They _____ to Brazil before.
   a have never been
   b haven't never gone

2 Complete the conversations. Use the simple past or present perfect form of the verbs in the box.

| not buy | drive | not eat | fly | go (x2) |
| have | meet | not read | not see | speak |

1 _____ you ever _____ in a helicopter?
2 I _____ you yesterday. I missed you!
3 I _____ any Russian novels. They're all so long!
4 Matt _____ never _____ sushi. He hates fish!
5 _____ she ever _____ a dog?
6 Jan and Mo _____ shopping last weekend, but they _____ anything.
7 _____ you _____ to the meeting, or _____ you _____ by train?
8 I _____ never _____ to Sue. What's she like?

3 Complete the conversation with the present perfect or simple past form of the verbs in parentheses.

Julia ¹_____ camping, Matteo? (you/ever/go)
Matteo Yes, I ²_____ last summer. (go)
Julia And ³_____ you _____ it? (enjoy)
Matteo It was awesome! ⁴_____ a fantastic time. (we/have)
Julia Who ⁵_____ with? (you/go)
Matteo I went with Sara and her family.
⁶_____ Sara? (you/meet)
Julia No, I ⁷_____ (have). How long ⁸_____ for? (you/go)
Matteo Five days. How about you? What ⁹_____ last summer? (you/do)
Julia I ¹⁰_____ around the U.S. with my cousin. (travel) It was amazing!

PRONUNCIATION: Vowels

4 ▶ 12.4 Match the past participles that have the same vowel sound. Listen, check, and repeat.

1 worn   _____   a won
2 written _____   b spoken
3 drunk   _____   c eaten
4 seen   _____   d driven
5 flown   _____   e met
6 read   _____   f bought

SKILLS 12D

WRITING: Writing and replying to an invitation

1 Complete the invitations and replies with the words in the box.

come   RSVP   sorry   make   having   can

2 Jan and Toni are talking on the phone. Complete their conversation with *a*, *an*, *the*, or – (no article).

Jan Hi Toni! Do you have [1]_____ recipe for pizza?
Toni Sure! Is it for [2]_____ housewarming party on Saturday?
Jan Yes – I love [3]_____ pizza, but I don't have a recipe for it.
Toni I can make some and bring it to your house before [4]_____ party.
Jan Really? That's so kind of you!
Toni No problem. It's 12 Pine Street, right?
Jan That's right! There's [5]_____ bus stop right in front. Thanks, Toni!

3 Reply to Jan and Bob's invitation. Use key phrases from exercise 1 and follow this structure:
- say hello
- say thanks
- decline the invitation
- say why
- say goodbye

4 Write an invitation to a party. Remember to include:
- the type of party
- the date and time
- your address
- other important information

71

12 REVIEW and PRACTICE

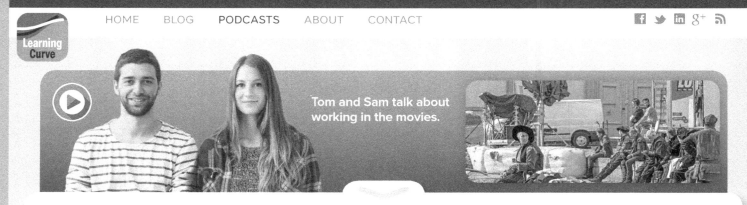

LISTENING

1 ▶ 12.5 Listen to the podcast about a job working in the movies. Check (✓) the adjectives you hear.

a fantastic ____
b cool ____
c exciting ____
d fun ____
e great ____
f amazing ____
g boring ____
h interesting ____

2 ▶ 12.5 Listen again and choose the correct options to complete the sentences.

1 What are "extras" in a movie?
  a They're the people in the background behind the actors. They don't speak.
  b They're the people behind the cameras. They help the director.
2 Does Mikael like being an extra?
  a Yes, he does. He loves it.
  b He doesn't mind it, but he says it's sometimes boring.

3 ▶ 12.5 Listen again. Are the sentences true (T) or false (F)?

1 Extras do the same thing every day. ____
2 They usually start work early in the morning. ____
3 They have to wait a lot. ____
4 Mikael doesn't like waiting. ____
5 He's met some famous people. ____
6 He was a teacher in a *Harry Potter* movie. ____
7 He's also been an extra on TV. ____
8 He loves working in film studios. ____
9 He'd like to work in an office. ____

READING

1 Read the blog on page 73 about a singing group.

1 What kind of music does Ivor's group sing?
  a music for young people
  b opera music
  c popular music
2 Who is the group for?
  a happy people
  b people the same age as Ivor
  c people who have been to the opera a lot

2 Read the sentences. Are they true (T), false (F), or doesn't say (DS)?

1 Most teenagers like opera. ____
2 Ivor has sung in 50 different operas. ____
3 Reports show that singing makes people feel tired. ____
4 Lots of people want to join Ivor's opera group. ____
5 It is difficult to become a member of the group. ____
6 The group will only sing songs from popular operas. ____
7 The group doesn't make any money from singing. ____
8 Being in the group has helped some people's confidence. ____

3 Circle the opinion adjectives in the blog.

72

REVIEW and PRACTICE 12

HOME   BLOG   PODCASTS   ABOUT   CONTACT

Tom and Sam look at making singing fun.

Singing for fun

What do you think when you hear the word "opera"? You might think "boring"! It's true that opera's not always popular with young people. Eighteen-year-old Ivor Golanski is trying to change that. In this special guest blog post, Ivor writes about his opera group "Singing for fun".

Many people my age have never been to the opera. I think that's sad and a little strange. I've been to about 50 operas in my life, and every time has been an awesome experience. So I decided that I wanted to start my own opera group for young people.

I've read reports that show how singing together can help people who are feeling tired or unhappy. When you sing, the body produces special chemicals that make you feel happy and relaxed. Singing together is fun, because when there are a lot of voices, it doesn't matter if you sing a wrong note – no one will hear it, so you won't feel stupid!

You don't have to be a great singer to join my group – but, of course, you can't have a terrible voice either! There are twenty members in the group now, and it's growing all the time. We always have a good time when we meet. Everyone works really hard, but we have a lot of fun together, as well.

We've already had a few concerts, where we sang songs from some well-known operas that lots of people know and like. We've sung in schools, at the city hall, and in our local theater. We haven't traveled to any other towns yet, but we'd like to. We're saving the money we make, and next year we'd like to go on a big tour.

Many people in the group tell me how singing has helped them in lots of ways. One member said, "Before I joined the opera group, I'd never been on stage. It was too scary! I'd only ever sung in the shower and thought I probably had a horrible voice. Now I feel much more confident about myself – my dream is to sing to a soccer stadium full of people!"

WRITING PRACTICE

WRITING: Planning and making notes

Last week, I went for a meal with my boyfriend. ¹*Before / Then* we went, I was really happy because I knew the restaurant was expensive and fashionable. I got dressed in my best clothes: a beautiful white dress and my best jewelry. ²*Then / First*, my boyfriend came to meet me at my house. It was a warm, sunny evening, and I felt fantastic.

Things didn't go well, though! The meal wasn't very good, and we had a terrible evening. ³*After / First*, the mushroom soup was cold. ⁴*Then / Before*, we had fish with rice and salad. The salad was terrible, too – I think it was a few days old.

⁵*Later / After* the meal, we had coffee. The waiter dropped a cup, and coffee went all over my white dress. I was so angry!

⁶*Later / First*, my boyfriend called me. He was really sorry! He sent flowers and chocolates to my house the next day. We are still together, but I don't want to go back to that restaurant – not ever!

1 Read Sandra's story. Choose the correct options for 1–6.

2 Number a–f in the order the things happened (1–6).

   a The waiter spilled coffee on Sandra. ____
   b Sandra ate some fish. ____
   c The soup wasn't good. ____
   d Sandra's boyfriend invited her to go for dinner. ____
   e Sandra's boyfriend sent presents to her. ____
   f Sandra's boyfriend called her. ____

3 Read the sentences. Complete the summary of Sandra's story.

   1 The story happened _____ week.
   2 At first, Sandra was happy because the _____ was expensive and fashionable.
   3 At the start of the story, Sandra's boyfriend met her at her _____.
   4 The meal wasn't good because the soup was _____ and the _____ was old.
   5 After the meal, Sandra was angry because she had _____ on her dress.
   6 Sandra and her boyfriend are still _____, but she doesn't want to go back to the restaurant again.

4 Think of a good or bad meal you ate. Write a story about it. Include the sequencers from exercise 1. Use the questions to make notes and plan your story.

   1 When did it happen?
   2 Where were you at the start?
   3 What were the main events?
   4 How did you feel at different times?
   5 What happened in the end?

WRITING PRACTICE

WRITING: Writing a description of a person

My favorite teacher is Mrs. Young. She's my music teacher. ¹_____ She has dark hair and happy eyes. She's always laughing! She's also a very good teacher, and she loves helping people. Mrs. Young lived with her aunt when she was a child. Her aunt was a musician and taught her to sing. Then, she learned to play the piano when she was three. ²_____ She was a student in college. At that time, she met her music band, The Dots. She played with them for many years. She stopped playing with her band. After that, she became a music teacher. She loved teaching young people, and she decided she wanted to teach music forever! She got a trumpet. After that, she started to play in a brass band. I admire Mrs. Young because she is a very good musician, and she works very hard. Her music classes are always fun. ³_____

By Mia

1 Read the description of Mrs. Young. Match the questions about her with notes a–e.

1 What does she teach? _____
2 What does she look like? _____
3 What did she learn to do when she was three years old? _____
4 Why does Mia admire her? _____
5 Why does Mia like her classes? _____

a always fun
b good musician, works hard
c to play the piano
d dark hair, happy eyes, always laughing
e music

2 Complete 1–3 in the description with the sentences. There is one extra sentence.

a I love singing and playing the guitar because she always teaches us that the most important thing is to enjoy music.
b She's a really friendly person and everyone likes her.
c Music is a very popular school subject in the U.S.
d Later, she started to learn the guitar in elementary school.

3 Join the sentences about Mrs. Young using a clause with *when*. Write two versions for each sentence.

Example
Mrs Young lived with her aunt when she was a child./When she was a child, Mrs Young lived with her aunt.

1 She was a student in college. At that time, she met her music band, The Dots.
_____

2 She stopped playing with her band. After that, she became a music teacher.
_____

3 She got a trumpet. That's when she started to play in a brass band.
_____

4 Write about a teacher you admire. Think about the questions below. Include two sentences with *when*.

1 What does this teacher teach?
2 What does he/she look like?
3 What do you know about his/her life and achievements?
4 Why do you admire this teacher?

78

WRITING PRACTICE

WRITING: Writing and replying to an invitation

I'm having a …
30th Birthday Trip!
I'd love you to join me!

We are going to go on a cruise in the Bahamas for three nights. We're going to stop in the capital, Nassau, and go sightseeing. The next day, we're going to go scuba diving on a small private island!

Where: Meet at the Miami cruise port on Dodge Island
When: June 18 – June 21
Please let me know if you can come!
Janine X
RSVP: janine95@pinkfish.com

Dear Janine,

Thanks so much for the invitation. What an exciting trip! I can definitely make it! I've never been to the Bahamas, but I would love to go there!

Can't wait to see you!

Lots of love,

Matt X

Dear Janine,

Thank you for the invitation. I'd love to come, but I don't have the money for the cruise. Also, I don't like traveling by boat because I get sick!

I hope you have a great time, and a very happy birthday.

Keep in touch.

Best wishes from Kylie

---

1 Read Janine's invitation and the two replies. Answer the questions.
   1 Where is Janine going? _____
   2 Who is going to go with her? _____
   3 Who can't go? _____

2 Complete each phrase with one word.
   1 I'm _____ a birthday trip!
   2 Hope you _____ come!
   3 Hope you can _____ it!
   4 _____ reply.
   5 I'm really _____, but we can't come.

3 Read Matt and Janine's online conversation. Choose the correct options to complete the sentences.

   Matt Hi Janine! I can't wait to go on the cruise.
   Janine I'm so happy you can come!
   Matt I'm going to bring some food for us to eat on the trip. Do you like ¹*a / – / the* chocolate?
   Janine I love it! Great idea. Thanks, Matt.
   Matt Is there ²*a / – / the* bus in Miami to the cruise port?
   Janine No, there isn't. Let's take ³*a / – / the* taxi. Where do you want to meet?
   Matt Let's meet at ⁴*a / – / the* mall, then, at 2.30! Bye!

4 Reply to Janine's invitation. Use key phrases from exercises 1 and 2.

5 Imagine you are having a birthday trip party. Answer the questions below. Then write an invitation to Janine. Remember to use key phrases from exercises 1 and 2.
   • Where are you going to go?
   • When are you going to go?
   • How are you going to get there?
   • Where are you going to stay?

NOTES

NOTES

Richmond

58 St Aldates
Oxford
OX1 1ST
United Kingdom

ISBN: 978-84-668-2595-5
Eleventh reprint: 2023
© Richmond / Santillana Global S.L. 2017

All rights reserved. No part of this book may be reproduced, stored in a retrieval system or transmitted in any form by any means, electronic, mechanical, photocopying, recording, or otherwise, without the prior permission in writing of the Publisher.

Publishing Director: Deborah Tricker
Publisher: Simone Foster
Media Publisher: Sue Ashcroft
Workbook Publisher: Luke Baxter
Editors: Debra Emmett, Tom Hadland, Fiona Hunt, Eleanor Clements, Helen Wendholt
Americanization: Deborah Goldblatt, Jennifer Wise
Proofreaders: Peter Anderson, Shannon Neill, Fiona Hunt
Design Manager: Lorna Heaslip
Cover Design: This Ain't Rock'n'Roll, London
Design & Layout: Lorna Heaslip, Oliver Hutton, 320 Design, ColArt Design
Photo Researcher: Magdalena Mayo
Learning Curve **video:** Mannic Media
Audio production: Eastern Sky Studios
App development: The Distance

We would also like to thank the following people for their valuable contribution to writing and developing the material:
Graham Fruen, Bob McLarty, Brigit Viney, Pamela Vittorio (Video Script Writer), Belen Fernandez (App Project Manager), Rob Sved (App Content Creator)

Illustrators:
Simon Clare, Richard Duckett, James Gibbs and Olvind Hovland c/o NB Illustration; Dermot Flynn c/o Dutch Uncle; John Goodwin, Joanna Kerr c/o New Division; John Holcroft; Neal c/o KJA Artists

Photos:
Alicia García; B. Balaguer; C. Pérez; J. Jaime; S. Enríquez; S. Padura; V. Atmán; 123RF; A. G. E. FOTOSTOCK/Pixtal, Fancy; ABB FOTÓGRAFOS; ALAMY/New York City, Johner Images, Josef Polc, Ira Berger, eye35, Geraint Lewis, David Crausby, Peter Usbeck, Nikreates, Joe Vogan, Urbanmyth, AF archive, Cultura RM, Phililp Quirk, Philip Scalia, AGF Srl, Jozef Polc, Roman Babakin, peter dazeley, Hero Images Inc., CRIBER PHOTO, Jim West, studiomonde, Ian Shaw, Zoonar GmbH, Thomas Cockrem, Blend Images, Ian Francis stock, Image Source, Olaf Doering, Peter Schatz, ONOKY - Photononstop, Roger Bamber, Tetra Images, Vadym Drobot, Aurora Photos, B Christopher, Brendan Duffy, Chloe Johnson, Pablo Paul, Y.Levy, Steven May, Michael Dwyer, STOCKFOLIO®, age fotostock, D. Hurst, Milan Machaty, aberCPC, Minkimo, View Stock, robertharding, Kevin Britland, Juan Aunion, REUTERS, Jochen Tack, Keith Leighton, Jorge Tutor, Peter Forsberg, Radharc Images, Fredrick Kippe, Danita Delimont, Francis Specker, Joerg Boethling, Loop Images Ltd, Wavebreak Media, Bill Bachmann, David Kilpatrick, Dzianis Apolka, Jan Halaska, Perry van Munster, Bernardo Galmarini, Jose Luis Stephens, Andrey Kekyalyaynen, Homer Sykes archive, Konstantin Kalishko, Jonathan Smith, dpa picture alliance, Cultura Creative (RF),

Jeff Greenberg 6 of 6, World History Archive, mauritius images GmbH, SIBSA Digital Pvt. Ltd., JTB Media Creation, INC., Henry Westheim Photography, Richard Wareham Fotografie, Sally and Richard Greenhill, The National Trust Photolibrary, epa european pressphoto agency b.v., Karol Kozlowski Premium RM Collection, Imagestate Media Partners Limited - Impact Photos, Universal Images Group North America LLC / DeAgostini, Magdalena Mayo; COMSTOCK; COVER; GETTY IMAGES SALES SPAIN/Erik Isakson/Tetra Images, Thinkstock/Jochen Sand, Toronto Star Archives, istock/Thinkstock, Adrian Weinbrecht, Photos.com Plus, TothGaborGyula, Paulo Fridman, Morsa Images, Alison Buck, stefanamer, Thinkstock, Jacobs Stock Photography, Bloomberg, Auscape; HIGHRES PRESS STOCK/AbleStock.com; I. PREYSLER; ISTOCKPHOTO/digitalskillet, sunstock, YvanDube, ImageGap, DarthArt, Getty Images Sales Spain; REX SHUTTERSTOCK/Max Lakner/BFA, Eugene Adebari, Tnt/BFA.com, Snap Stills, Howard/ANL; SETH POPPEL YEARBOOK LIBRARY; SHUTTERSTOCK/Sky Designs, Dean Drobot, Fotocrisis; STOCKBYTE; Jim Benjaminson Collections via the Plymouth Bulletin; Samsung; SERIDEC PHOTOIMAGENES CD; J. Lucas; M. Sánchez; Prats i Camps; 123RF; ALAMY/Blend Images, INTERFOTO, REUTERS, Keith Homan, MBI, imageBROKER, Jose Luis Suerte, Harold Smith, Ian Allenden, Peter Horree, MS Bretherton, Pulsar Images, andy lane, Nano Calvo, Radharc Images, Westend61 GmbH, Colin Underhill, Gianni Muratore, Mary Evans Picture Library, Michael Wheatley, Alibi Productions, a-plus image bank, ONOKY - Photononstop, Directphoto Collection, Arterra Picture Library, Martin Thomas Photography, Agencja Fotograficzna Caro, Cathy Topping, Blend Images - BUILT Content, Geraint Lewis; GETTY IMAGES SALES SPAIN/Thinkstock; I. PREYSLER; ISTOCKPHOTO/Getty Images Sales Spain; SHUTTERSTOCK; SHUTTERSTOCK NETHERLANDS,B.V.; SOUTHWEST NEWS/Leicester Mercury; ARCHIVO SANTILLANA

Cover Photo: istockphoto/wundervisuals

We would like to thank the following reviewers for their valuable feedback which has made Personal Best possible. We extend our thanks to the many teachers and students not mentioned here.
Brad Bawtinheimer, Manuel Hidalgo, Paulo Dantas, Diana Bermúdez, Laura Gutiérrez, Hardy Griffin, Angi Conti, Christopher Morabito, Hande Kokce, Jorge Lobato, Leonardo Mercato, Mercilinda Ortiz, Wendy López

The Publisher has made every effort to trace the owner of copyrighted material; however, the Publisher will correct any involuntary omission at the earliest opportunity.

Printed in Brazil by Forma Certa Gráfica Digital
Lote: 798932
Cod: 290525955